SOUPS

13-Digit ISBN: 978-1-60433-893-5
10-Digit ISBN: 1-60433-893-8

This book may be ordered by mail from the publisher. Please include $5.99 for postage and handling. Please support your local bookseller first!

Books published by Cider Mill Press Book Publishers are available at special discounts for bulk purchases in the United States by corporations, institutions, and other organizations. For more information, please contact the publisher.

Cider Mill Press Book Publishers

"Where Good Books Are Ready for Press"

PO Box 454
12 Spring Street
Kennebunkport, Maine 04046

Visit us online! www.cidermillpress.com

Typography: Bushcraft, Adobe Garamond, Clarendon, Fenway Park, Sentinel Black, Helvetica Round, and Neutraface 2

Image Credits: Image Credits: Photographs on pages 4-5, 6-7, 10-11, 21, 26-27, 28-29, 31, 39, 66-67, 68-69, 97, 112-113, 114-115, 146-147, 148-149, 151, 168-169, 170-171, 190-191, 192-193, 212-213, 214-215, 217, 232-233, 253, 269, and 280-281 are used under official license from Shutterstock.com.

All other images courtesy of Cider Mill Press Book Publishers LLC.

Printed in China
2 3 4 5 6 7 8 9 0

SOUPS

Over 100 INTERNATIONALLY INSPIRED SOUPS *and* STEWS

DEREK BISSONNETTE

CIDER MILL PRESS

BOOK
PUBLISHERS
KENNEBUNKPORT, MAINE

Contents

Introduction

THE ONLY UNIVERSAL DISH

The world contains countless cuisines, techniques, and ingredients. But there is one thing that bonds them all—every single culture has some form of soup. They can be thick or thin, can feature seafood, meat, or vegetables, and can even be clarified with gastronomic ingredients, as with consommé.

Whatever they contain, soups have been around for some time. Broths show up in the historical record around the year 1000 CE, and in the 15th century, soup dishes known as potages became a staple in the lives of peasants around the world. In fact, soups are such a vital part of what we eat that the word stems from *suppare*, the same Latin word that is the origin of "supper."

IN THE BEGINNING

It is commonly held that cooking food was an accident, stumbled upon sometime after mankind discovered fire 1.8 million years ago. This happy accident launched a revolution that is still underway.

The best way to cook, and the most efficient use of fire's precious heat, is boiling. Boiling kills any potential parasites, preserves nutrients, increases the amount of antioxidants, and makes things easier to chew. Most importantly, the cooking liquid retains ingredients' tasty juices, which would be lost if cooked over an open flame.

But finding containers that could support a boiling meal was a challenge early on. Prehistoric cooks utilized a technique called pitcooking: digging a hole in the ground, building a fire within, and covering the hole so that it functioned as a rudimentary oven. This made it possible to steam the evening meal, but boiling remained elusive. Eventually, hollowed out rocks, turtle shells, or large pieces of bark were used for boiling. And, on occasion, the animal itself was used as a pot.

Eventually, humans discovered how to fire clay, and vessels that could hold liquid as it cooked became commonplace. At first, these pots were cooked directly in the fire, but over time handles were added, allowing the cook to control the temperature by altering the pot's distance from the heat source.

Clay pots were a big step, but the true revolution came once humans learned to work with metal, leading to the cooking utensils we use today.

THE ORIGINAL COMFORT FOOD

Soups became associated with promoting health—so much so that they essentially were the health care system until the advent of modern medicine. Medical textbooks of the time read more like diet books. In China, snakes were used to make soups that were believed to help with joint pain. The meat of a strong animal was thought to strengthen a weak man. And then, there is the age-old belief in chicken soup's healing capabilities. This stems from the Ancient Greeks, who recommended the meat of hens and roosters—and broth made from their bones—for many treatments.

As it turns out, this was not just an ancient superstition. Chicken actually contains a compound called carnosine that slows or blocks the migration of white blood cells, which reduces the amount of inflammation in the respiratory tract during the common cold. Researchers have also found that chicken soup may improve one's ability to deflect a virus and weaken it upon entry into the body. On top of all this, it also allows mucus to escape the body more freely, which keeps airways clear and eases the effects of congestion. So, unsurprisingly enough, it turns out that the Ancient Greeks—and your mother—have it right.

THE FIRST RECIPES

History documents that peasants ate the same potage for every meal, using ingredients that were easily accessible. The wealthy, however, had a vast number of dishes at their disposal. *De re Coquinaria (On the Subject of Cooking)*, a collection of Roman recipes gathered from the 1st century to the 5th, shows that they enjoyed a large variety of soups featuring a number of exotic ingredients.

The first-known English cookbook, *Forme of Cury*, was written by the master cooks of King Richard II in the late 14th century. This text contains a number of soup-like recipes, and a number of dishes referred to as broths. It also features the preparation for decadent items such as whale, crane, seal, and porpoise.

The earliest German cooking manuscript, *Ein Buch von guter spise* (The Book of Good Food), was composed in the mid-1300s. Included in the text is a recipe for *Ein spise von bonen* (a food of beans), which features a broth consisting of beer, vinegar, caraway seeds, and ground saffron.

While soup was always something people were interested in, it wasn't until the 17th century that the culinary arts really developed. This development was due to an increased knowledge of vegetables and grains, wider access to a larger variety of ingredients, and an explosion in the publication of cookbooks.

SOUP TODAY

In times of emotional stress, soup can evoke feelings of warmth, happiness, satisfaction, and human connection.

Soups also make for a great amuse-bouche or intermezzo (palate cleanser) at a restaurant, allowing the chef to keep the customer happy and entertained while they work through a five-course, prix fixe menu.

It's enjoyable for the customer, and it's a life-saver for the kitchen. With that many courses, there's bound to be a mistake or two once the pace picks up. By having a lovely, inventive soup on hand, chefs can buy themselves time by sending out a little something—and the goodwill this extra, special taste engenders doesn't hurt, either.

Not to say that soup can't be more than just a distraction. It works for lunch, dinner, and dessert. On a crisp fall day it's the perfect accompaniment to a warm sweater and a fresh roll with butter.

As long as the soup's good, that's heaven.

Stock

A stock is traditionally a base for broths and consommés made from the bones and carcasses of a protein (vegetable stock is an obvious exception), and often features vegetables and aromatics. It is important that the bones are cooked for hours so that every last bit of flavor makes its way into the stock.

There are white stocks and brown stocks. The former is made from the bones of white proteins, such as chicken, and lighter colored vegetables. Brown stocks are made from the bones of darker meats, such as beef.

In French cuisine, a basic stock is referred to as a *fonds*, which translates to "foundation." Some soups require the solid foundation a stock can provide, while others need nothing more than the proper combination of ingredients, time, and patience.

When you're preparing a stock, soup, or stew, resist the temptation to tinker and leave your seasoning until the end. Since there are plenty of naturally occuring flavors in your ingredients, these will enter the soup as it cooks. Think of time and heat as doing the seasoning for you, as the flavor of almost every soup is indicative of the time invested.

Veal, Beef, or Lamb Stock

YIELD: 6 QUARTS • ACTIVE TIME: 30 MINUTES • TOTAL TIME: 6½ HOURS

When making a brown stock, try to use veal bones, as they have a smoother taste than beef. It also creates tender, lighter, and finer stock than pure beef. That said, beef bones are much cheaper and more accessible than veal bones, so these will often be what you're working with.

INGREDIENTS

10 lbs. veal, beef, or lamb bones

½ cup vegetable oil

1 leek, trimmed and cut into 1-inch pieces

1 large yellow onion, unpeeled, root cleaned, cut into 1-inch pieces

2 large carrots, peeled and cut into 1-inch pieces

1 celery stalk with leaves, cut into 1-inch pieces

10 quarts water

8 sprigs parsley

5 sprigs thyme

2 bay leaves

1 teaspoon black peppercorns

1 teaspoon salt

8 oz. tomato paste

1 Preheat oven to 350°F.

2 Lay the bones on a flat baking tray, place in oven, and cook for 30 to 45 minutes, until they are golden brown. Remove and set aside.

3 Meanwhile, in a large stockpot, add the vegetable oil and warm over low heat. Add the vegetables and cook until any additional moisture has evaporated, to concentrate the flavors.

4 Add the water to the stock pot. Add the bones, aromatics, spices, and tomato paste to the stockpot, raise heat to high, and bring to a boil.

5 Reduce heat so that the stock simmers and cook for a minimum of 2 hours. Skim fat and impurities from the top as the stock cooks. Cook until the desired flavor is achieved, around 4 to 5 hours.

6 When the stock is finished cooking, strain through a fine strainer or cheesecloth. Place stock in refrigerator to chill.

7 Once cool, skim the fat layer from the top and discard. Use immediately, refrigerate, or freeze.

TIPS:
- STOCKS CAN STAY IN A FREEZER FOR UP TO SIX MONTHS.
- WHEN USING LAMB BONES IN A BROWN STOCK, USE HALF LAMB AND HALF VEAL OR BEEF BONES. THE LAMB BONES HAVE A PARTICULARLY STRONG FLAVOR, WHICH CAN OVERWHELM A SOUP IF YOU ARE NOT CAREFUL.
- THIS IS A LARGE RECIPE, WHICH CAN EASILY BE REDUCED TO HALF OR ONE-QUARTER THE AMOUNT. HOWEVER, IT'S ALWAYS A GOOD IDEA TO HAVE EXCESS STOCK STORED IN THE FREEZER.

Chicken Stock

YIELD: 6 QUARTS • ACTIVE TIME: 30 MINUTES • TOTAL TIME: 6½ HOURS

Chicken stock falls under the category of a white stock. As with most of these stocks, the more time, the merrier. If you're unsure whether it's ready, it's probably not. Cook until you would consider eating it on its own. This recipe will also work with duck and turkey as the protein.

INGREDIENTS

10 lbs. chicken carcasses and/or stewing chicken pieces

½ cup vegetable oil

1 leek, trimmed and cut into 1-inch pieces

1 large yellow onion, unpeeled, root cleaned, cut into 1-inch pieces

2 large carrots, peeled and cut into 1-inch pieces

1 celery stalk with leaves, cut into 1-inch pieces

10 quarts water

1 teaspoon salt

8 sprigs parsley

5 sprigs thyme

2 bay leaves

1 teaspoon black peppercorns

1 Preheat oven to 350°F. Separate the bones from the meat of the carcasses and lay the bones on a flat baking tray. Place the bones in the oven and cook for 30 to 45 minutes until golden brown. Remove and set aside.

3 Meanwhile, in a large stockpot, add the vegetable oil and warm over low heat. Add the vegetables and cook until any additional moisture has evaporated to concentrate the flavors.

4 Add the water and the salt to the stock pot. Add the chicken carcasses and/or stewing pieces, the aromatics, and the peppercorns to the stockpot, raise heat to high, and bring to a boil.

5 Reduce heat so that the stock simmers and cook for a minimum of 2 hours. Skim fat and impurities from the top as the stock cooks. Cook until the desired flavor is achieved, around 4 to 5 hours.

6 When the stock is finished cooking, strain through a fine strainer or cheesecloth. Place stock in refrigerator to chill. Once cool, skim the fat layer from the top and discard. Use immediately, refrigerate, or freeze.

Crab Stock

This stock is made with cooked crab. If using raw crab, combine all the ingredients except for the crab in the stockpot and bring to a boil. Add the crab legs and cook for 8 minutes, remove, and submerge in ice water. Reduce the heat so that the stock simmers, remove the crab meat from the shells and return the shells to the stock.

1 In a large stockpot, add the vegetable oil and warm over low heat. Add the vegetables and cook until any additional moisture has evaporated to concentrate the flavors.

2 Add the crab shells, the remaining ingredients, and enough water to cover the shells by 1-inch.

3 Raise heat to high and bring to a boil. Reduce heat so that the stock simmers. Skim fat and impurities from the top as the stock cooks for at least 4 hours total.

4 When the stock is finished cooking, strain through a fine strainer or cheesecloth. Place stock in refrigerator to chill.

5 Once cool, skim the fat layer from the top and discard. Use immediately, refrigerate, or freeze.

INGREDIENTS

2 tablespoons vegetable oil

1 onion, chopped

1 carrot, peeled, roughly chopped

1 celery stalk, roughly chopped

3 lbs. crab legs, cooked in the shell, meat removed and reserved, shells used in stock

½ cup white wine

4 tablespoons tomato paste

2 sprigs thyme

2 sprigs parsley

3 sprigs tarragon

1 bay leaf

½ teaspoon black peppercorns

1 teaspoon salt

8 cardamom pods

Water, as needed

Dashi Stock

Dashi stock has two very flavorful ingredients, one of which goes bitter if cooked at too high a temperature. Because of this, it's a quick and easy stock to make. You can freeze any excess, though it works best if made close to the preparation of the soup. Kombu is edible dried kelp and bonito is a dried and fermented fish.

INGREDIENTS

8 cups cold water

2 oz. kombu

1 cup bonito flakes

1 In a medium saucepan, add the water and the kombu. Soak for 20 minutes, remove the kombu, and score gently with a knife.

2 Return the kombu to the saucepan and bring to a boil.

3 Remove the kombu as soon as the water boils so that the stock doesn't become bitter.

4 Add the bonito flakes and return to a boil. Turn off heat and let stand.

5 Strain through a fine sieve and chill in the refrigerator.

Ham Stock

YIELD: 4 CUPS • ACTIVE TIME: 15 MINUTES • TOTAL TIME: 1 HOUR AND 15 MINUTES

While the standard pork stock uses bones, this one uses ham instead. If you wish to go the traditional route, you can substitute pork bones and follow the recipe for Veal, Beef, or Lamb Stock (see page 12) instead.

1 Combine all ingredients in a stockpot and bring to a boil.

2 Reduce heat so that the stock simmers and cook for 1 hour. Strain stock through a fine sieve and chill in the refrigerator.

INGREDIENTS

12 oz. ham

6 cups water

2 garlic cloves, minced

1 onion, chopped

1 bay leaf

1 sprig thyme

Fish Stock

YIELD: 6 QUARTS • ACTIVE TIME: 20 MINUTES • TOTAL TIME: 2½ HOURS

Traditionally only white fish should be used for this stock, as it is a good way to avoid incorporating extra oil into the recipe, and fish like tuna and salmon can overpower the stock. That said, if using this stock for a creamed or thickened soup, don't hesitate to use a salmon carcass if you have one on hand.

INGREDIENTS

½ cup vegetable oil

1 leek, trimmed and cut into 1-inch pieces

1 large yellow onion, unpeeled, root cleaned, cut into 1-inch pieces

2 large carrots, peeled and cut into 1-inch pieces

1 celery stalk with leaves, cut into 1-inch pieces

10 lbs. white fish bodies

8 sprigs parsley

5 sprigs thyme

2 bay leaves

1 teaspoon black peppercorns

1 teaspoon salt

10 quarts water

1 In a large stockpot, add the vegetable oil and warm over low heat. Add the vegetables and cook until any additional moisture has evaporated to concentrate the flavors.

2 Add the white fish bodies, the aromatics, peppercorns, salt, and the water to the pot.

3 Raise heat to high and bring to a boil. Reduce heat so that the stock simmers and cook for a minimum of 2 hours, skimming fat and impurities from the top as the stock cooks.

4 When the stock is finished cooking, strain through a fine strainer or cheesecloth. Place stock in the refrigerator to chill.

5 Once cool, skim the fat layer from the top and discard. Use immediately, refrigerate, or freeze.

Lobster Stock

YIELD: 8 CUPS • ACTIVE TIME: 20 MINUTES • TOTAL TIME: 5½ HOURS

This stock is made with the cooked bodies and shells of the lobster, which are very flavorful when roasted. The V8™ helps add a nice touch of red and even more flavor. When straining this stock, be sure to press on the lobster bodies with a ladle for every last bit of flavor.

1 Preheat oven to 350°F.

2 Lay the lobster bodies on a baking tray, place in oven, and cook for 30 to 45 minutes. Remove and set aside.

3 Meanwhile, in a large stockpot, add the vegetable oil and warm over low heat. Add the root vegetables and cook until any additional moisture has evaporated to concentrate the flavors.

4 Add the lobster bodies, tomatoes, V8™, herbs, garlic, and white wine to the stockpot. Add enough water to cover the shells, raise heat to high, and bring to a boil. Reduce heat so that the stock simmers and cook for a minimum of 2 hours and a maximum of 4 hours. Skim fat and impurities from the top as the stock cooks.

When the stock is finished cooking, strain through fine strainer or cheesecloth. Place stock in the refrigerator to chill.

Once cool, skim the fat layer from the top and discard. Use immediately, refrigerate, or freeze.

INGREDIENTS

5 lbs. lobster shells and bodies

2 tablespoons vegetable oil

1 lb. mixed root vegetables (carrot, leek, onion, celery), chopped

10 tomatoes, chopped

1 cup V8™

1 bunch thyme

1 bunch parsley

1 bunch tarragon

1 bunch dill

1 garlic clove

2 cups white wine

Water, as needed

Vegetable Stock

When making a vegetable stock, it's best to avoid starchy vegetables, such as potatoes, as they will make the stock cloudy. Also try to avoid very colorful vegetables, such as beets, as their color will leech into the stock. This stock can be used to replace the meat stock in a majority of the recipes in this book.

INGREDIENTS

2 tablespoons vegetable oil

2 large leeks, trimmed

2 large carrots, peeled and sliced

2 celery stalks, sliced

2 large onions, sliced

3 garlic cloves, unpeeled and smashed

2 sprigs parsley

2 sprigs thyme

1 bay leaf

½ teaspoon black peppercorns

Salt, to taste

8 cups water

In a large stockpot, add the vegetable oil and the vegetables and cook over low heat until any additional moisture has evaporated to concentrate the flavors.

Add the garlic, aromatics, peppercorns, salt, and water. Raise heat to high and bring to a boil. Reduce heat so that the soup simmers and cook for 2 hours. Skim fat and impurities from the top as the stock cooks.

When the stock is finished cooking, strain through a fine strainer or cheesecloth. Place stock in the refrigerator to chill.

Once cool, skim the fat layer from the top and discard. Use immediately, refrigerate, or freeze.

Pasta

The recipes in this chapter focus on everyone's favorite: pastas and noodles. These recipes mostly use dried pastas and noodles, as dried pasta will give these soups a better mouthfeel. You can make your own pasta and dry it, of course, if you're looking to add a homemade touch to your next meal.

Broken Pasta Soup

YIELD: 4 SERVINGS • ACTIVE TIME: 20 MINUTES • TOTAL TIME: 45 MINUTES

This is a great healthy soup, which becomes much easier to eat with the broken pasta.

INGREDIENTS

2 teaspoons extra virgin olive oil

1 onion, chopped

2 garlic cloves, minced

2 carrots, peeled and chopped

1 zucchini, seeds removed, chopped

4 celery stalks, chopped

2 (14 oz.) cans stewed tomatoes

4 cups vegetable stock (see page 25)

2 oz. spaghetti, broken into 2-inch pieces

2 tablespoons parsley, leaves removed and chopped

Salt and pepper, to taste

Basil Pesto, to serve (see page 180)

1 In a medium saucepan, add the oil and cook over medium heat until warm. Add the onion and cook for 5 minutes, or until soft. Add the garlic, carrots, zucchini, and celery, and cook for 5 minutes. Add the tomatoes and stock, and bring to a boil.

2 Reduce heat so that the soup simmers and cook for 15 minutes.

3 Add the spaghetti and cook for 8 to 10 minutes, or until the pasta is tender.

4 Stir in the parsley, season with salt and pepper, and serve in warm bowls with Basil Pesto.

Vietnamese Pho

YIELD: 4 SERVINGS • ACTIVE TIME: 30 MINUTES • TOTAL TIME: 3½ HOURS

Pho is a soup consisting of broth, rice noodles, spices, and either beef or chicken, and is a popular street food in Vietnam that has slowly spread to the rest of the world.

1 Preheat oven to 350°F. Place the bones in the oven and roast for 20 minutes, or until golden brown. Meanwhile, char the onion and ginger over an open flame.

2 Place all of the spices in a nonstick pan and cook over medium heat for 2 to 3 minutes, until they become fragrant.

3 Add the bones, charred onion and ginger, spices, cilantro, and the water in a large saucepan and bring to a boil.

4 Reduce heat so that the soup simmers and cook for 3 hours.

5 Strain the soup into a clean pot. Season with fish sauce, hoisin, black pepper, and Sriracha. Return to a simmer.

6 Place the rice noodles into a bowl and cover with boiling water. Let soak for 4 minutes, or according to manufacturer's instructions.

7 Place the rice noodles into warm bowls. Ladle the soup over the noodles and garnish with sliced jalapeño, bean sprouts, lime wedges, and Thai basil.

INGREDIENTS

2 lbs. beef or chicken bones

1 small yellow onion, halved

1-inch piece ginger, unpeeled

2 cinnamon sticks

3 star anise

2 cardamom pods, seeds removed and chopped

1 tablespoon black peppercorns

5 cloves

1 tablespoon coriander seed

1 tablespoon fennel seed

1 cup cilantro, leaves and stems

8 cups water

1 tablespoon fish sauce

1 tablespoon hoisin

Black pepper, to taste

1 teaspoon Sriracha

3 oz. rice noodles

Jalapeño, sliced, for garnish

Bean sprouts, for garnish

Lime wedges, for garnish

Thai basil, for garnish

Chicken Liver and Pasta Soup with Baked Herb Baguette Slices

YIELD: 4 SERVINGS • ACTIVE TIME: 25 MINUTES • TOTAL TIME: 1 HOUR

Chicken livers can be purchased at most large grocery stores, and can be frozen for later use.

1 Add the oil and butter to a medium saucepan and cook over medium-high heat until warm. Add the chicken livers and garlic and sauté for 3 minutes, or until the chicken livers are golden brown.

2 Add the wine and cook until it evaporates. Stir in the herbs and cook for 2 minutes. Remove pan from heat and set aside.

3 In a large saucepan, add the chicken stock and bring to a boil. Reduce heat so that the stock simmers, add the peas, and cook for 5 minutes.

4 While the peas are cooking, preheat the oven to 350°F. To make the Baked Herbed Baguette Slices, place the herbs and olive oil in a bowl and mix until combined. Place the slices of baguette on a baking sheet, drizzle with the herbed olive oil, season with salt and pepper, and bake for 10 minutes or until golden brown.

5 Return the soup to a boil and add the farfalle. Reduce the heat so that the stock simmers and cook for 10 minutes, until the pasta is al dente.

6 Add the chicken livers and scallions and simmer for 3 minutes. Season with salt and pepper, ladle into warm bowls, and serve with Baked Herbed Baguette Slices.

INGREDIENTS

For the Chicken Liver and Pasta Soup

1 tablespoon extra virgin olive oil

1 tablespoon unsalted butter

½ cup chicken livers, cut into ¼-inch pieces

4 garlic cloves, minced

2 tablespoons white wine

3 sprigs parsley, leaves removed and chopped

3 sprigs marjoram, leaves removed and chopped

3 sprigs sage, leaves removed and chopped

1 sprig thyme, leaves removed and chopped

6 basil leaves, chopped

6 cups chicken stock (see page 14)

2 cups peas

1 cup farfalle pasta

3 scallions, white part only, sliced

Salt and pepper, to taste

For the Baked Herbed Baguette Slices

1 teaspoon parsley, chopped

1 teaspoon marjoram, chopped

1 teaspoon sage, chopped

1 teaspoon thyme, chopped

1 teaspoon basil, chopped

1 cup extra virgin olive oil

Baguette, sliced into 8 pieces, ¼-inch thick

Salt and pepper, to taste

Five-Spice and Chicken Ramen

YIELD: 4 SERVINGS • ACTIVE TIME: 15 MINUTES • TOTAL TIME: 1 HOUR

Here is a quick, simple ramen that is perfect for a cold day.

INGREDIENTS

6 cups chicken stock (see page 14)

4 garlic cloves, minced

2-inch piece of ginger, minced

½ cup soy sauce

2 teaspoons Worcestershire sauce

1 teaspoon five-spice powder

⅛ teaspoon chili powder

1 tablespoon sugar, optional

Salt and pepper, to taste

2 tablespoons sesame oil

4 cups water

8 oz. udon noodles

2 chicken breasts, cut into 1-inch cubes

4 eggs

1 cup corn kernels

1 cup spinach

8 scallion greens, for garnish

1 sheet nori, torn, for garnish

1 In a medium saucepan, add the chicken stock, garlic, ginger, soy sauce, Worcestershire sauce, five-spice powder, and chili powder and bring to a boil.

2 Reduce heat so that the soup simmers and cook for 5 minutes. Turn off the heat and let stand. Season with sugar, salt, and pepper. Add the sesame oil to a medium sauté pan and cook over medium heat.

3 Bring the water to boil in a medium saucepan. Add the udon noodles and cook according to manufacturer's instructions.

4 Add the chicken to the sauté pan and cook for 8 minutes, or until browned on all sides.

5 To hardboil the eggs, bring enough water to cover the eggs by at least 1 inch to a boil in a medium saucepan. Once boiling, reduce to a simmer, add the eggs, and cook for 10 minutes.

6 Remove, refresh in iced water, and leave for 10 minutes. Once cooled, peel, slice in half, and set aside.

7 Add the corn kernels to the chicken and cook for 2 minutes. Add the cooked udon noodles and spinach and cook for 1 minute.

8 Strain the broth through a fine sieve, and discard the solids. Place the broth in a clean pan and bring to a boil.

9 Place the udon noodles in warm bowls. Pour the broth over the top and garnish with the hardboiled eggs, scallions, and nori.

Italian Wedding Soup

YIELD: 4 SERVINGS • ACTIVE TIME: 20 MINUTES • TOTAL TIME: 1 HOUR

The term wedding soup comes from the phrase *minestra maritata,* which means "married soup," a reference to the combination of leafy greens and meat.

INGREDIENTS

For the Meatballs

12 oz. ground chicken

⅓ cup panko bread crumbs

1 garlic clove, minced

2 tablespoons parsley, leaves removed and chopped

¼ cup Parmesan cheese, grated

1 tablespoon milk

1 egg, beaten

⅛ teaspoon fennel seeds

⅛ teaspoon red pepper flakes

½ teaspoon paprika

Salt and pepper, to taste

For the Italian Wedding Soup

2 tablespoons extra virgin olive oil

1 onion, chopped

2 carrots, peeled and diced

1 celery stalk, diced

6 cups chicken stock (see page 14)

¼ cup white wine

½ cup tubetini pasta

2 tablespoons dill, chopped

6 oz. baby spinach

Salt and pepper, to taste

Parmesan cheese, grated, for garnish

1 To make the meatballs, preheat the oven to 350°F. Add all the ingredients to a bowl and mix with a fork until well-combined.

2 Divide the mixture into 16 balls, roll with your hands until nice and round, and then place on a baking tray. Bake for 20 to 25 minutes, until nicely browned and cooked through. Remove from oven and set aside.

3 To prepare the soup, in a medium saucepan, add the olive oil and cook over medium heat until warm. Add the onion, carrots, and celery and cook for 5 minutes, or until soft. Add the stock and the wine, and bring to a boil.

4 Reduce heat so that the soup simmers, add the pasta, and cook for 8 minutes. Add the cooked meatballs and simmer for 5 minutes. Add the dill and the spinach and cook for 2 minutes, or until the spinach has wilted.

5 Season with salt and pepper, ladle into warm bowls, and garnish with Parmesan.

Tomato Soup with Cheddar Cheese Dumplings

YIELD: 4 SERVINGS • ACTIVE TIME: 30 MINUTES • TOTAL TIME: 1 HOUR

Do you like tomato soup and grilled cheese? Then you are certain to love this soup that puts a slightly different twist on this classic.

INGREDIENTS

For the Tomato Soup

2 tablespoons unsalted butter

1 onion, chopped

2 lbs. tomatoes, chopped

2 carrots, peeled and chopped

5 cups chicken stock (see page 14)

2 tablespoons parsley leaves, chopped, plus more for garnish

½ teaspoon thyme leaves, chopped

6 tablespoons heavy cream, plus more for garnish

Salt and pepper, to taste

Parmesan cheese, shaved, for garnish

For the Cheddar Cheese Dumplings

¾ cup all-purpose flour

1 teaspoon baking powder

¼ teaspoon salt

⅓ cup sharp cheddar cheese, grated

½ cup buttermilk

3 tablespoons parsley, leaves removed and chopped

1 To make the soup, place the butter in a large saucepan and cook over medium heat until melted. Add the onion and cook for 5 minutes, or until soft.

2 Stir in the tomatoes, carrots, chicken stock, parsley, and thyme, reduce to low and simmer for 20 minutes, or until the vegetables are tender. Transfer the soup to a food processor, puree, and then pass through a fine sieve.

3 Return the soup to the pan and add the cream. Reheat gently, season with salt and pepper, and let simmer while you prepare the Cheddar Cheese Dumplings.

4 Combine the flour, baking powder, and salt in a mixing bowl. Add the cheddar cheese, buttermilk, and parsley, and mix with a fork until a dough forms.

5 When the dough becomes thick, use your hands and knead it until it is nice and smooth. Add water or flour, as necessary. Drop tablespoon-sized dumplings into the simmering tomato soup.

6 Once all the dough has been incorporated, simmer for 10 minutes. Turn off the heat and let stand for a few minutes. Ladle into warm bowls, and garnish with Parmesan, a splash of heavy cream, and parsley.

Chicken Parm Soup

YIELD: 4 SERVINGS • ACTIVE TIME: 20 MINUTES • TOTAL TIME: 1 HOUR

By turning this famous Italian-American dish into a soup, your work in the kitchen is certain to garner a few devotees.

1 In a medium saucepan, add the oil and warm over medium-high heat. Add the chicken and cook for 5 minutes, while turning, until golden brown.

2 Add the onion and garlic and cook for 5 minutes, or until the onion is soft.

3 Add the red pepper flakes, tomato paste, tomatoes, and stock, and bring to a boil.

4 Reduce heat so that the soup simmers and cook for 10 minutes.

5 Add the penne and cook for 12 minutes. Add the mozzarella and Parmesan and stir until melted. Season with salt and pepper, ladle into bowls, and garnish with basil and Parmesan.

INGREDIENTS

2 tablespoons extra virgin olive oil

2 chicken breasts, cut into ½-inch pieces

1 onion, chopped

2 garlic cloves, minced

1 teaspoon crushed red pepper flakes

¼ cup tomato paste

1 (14 oz.) can stewed tomatoes, diced

6 cups chicken stock (see page 14)

2 cups penne

2 cups mozzarella cheese, grated

1 cup Parmesan cheese, grated, plus more for garnish

Salt and pepper, to taste

Basil, chopped, for garnish

Chickpea and Pasta Soup

YIELD: 4 SERVINGS • ACTIVE TIME: 15 MINUTES • TOTAL TIME: 10½ HOURS

This simple Italian soup is perfect for your vegan friends or family members. Ditalini is a small, tube-shaped pasta.

INGREDIENTS

1¼ cup dried chickpeas, soaked overnight

6 cups water

1 tablespoon dried kombu

3 garlic cloves

2 tablespoons extra virgin olive oil, plus more for garnish

2 sprigs rosemary, 1 left whole, 1 leaves removed and chopped

1 cup ditalini pasta

Salt and pepper, to taste, plus more pepper for garnish

Crusty bread, to serve

1 Rinse the chickpeas and then place in a medium saucepan. Cover with the water, add the kombu and the cloves of garlic, and bring to a simmer. Cook for 2 hours, or until the chickpeas are nice and tender.

2 Reserve ¹⁄4 of the cooked chickpeas. Transfer the remaining contents of the saucepan to a food processor and puree.

3 In a medium heavy-bottom pan, add the olive oil and warm over medium-high heat.

4 Place the whole rosemary sprig into the pan and cook for a few minutes until soft and fragrant. Remove the rosemary sprig and discard. Add the chickpea puree and reserved chickpeas. Add the pasta and cook for 10 minutes. If the soup becomes too thick, add more water.

5 Add the chopped rosemary, season with salt and pepper, and ladle into warm bowls. Garnish with a splash of olive oil and black pepper, and serve with crusty bread.

Leftover Turkey Pasta Soup

YIELD: 4 SERVINGS • ACTIVE TIME: 15 MINUTES • TOTAL TIME: 40 MINUTES

Everybody loves Thanksgiving, and everybody enjoys the day after even more. Make that day even better with the help of this soup. If you want to make turkey stock, follow the Chicken Stock recipe.

1 In a medium saucepan, warm oil over medium heat. Add the onion, celery, and carrots and cook for 5 minutes, or until soft.

2 Add the stock, bay leaf, and rosemary and bring to a boil.

3 Reduce heat so that the soup simmers and cook for 10 minutes.

4 Add the orzo and simmer for 8 to 10 minutes, or until the pasta is tender.

5 Add the turkey meat and parsley. Season with salt and pepper and serve in warm bowls.

INGREDIENTS

1 tablespoon extra virgin olive oil

1 onion, chopped

2 celery stalks, chopped

2 carrots, peeled and chopped

6 cups chicken stock (see page 14)

1 bay leaf

1 teaspoon rosemary, leaves removed and chopped

½ cup orzo

2 cups leftover turkey meat, chopped

1 teaspoon parsley, leaves removed and chopped

Salt and pepper, to taste

Old Fashioned Chicken Broth and Dumpling Soup

YIELD: 4 SERVINGS • ACTIVE TIME: 30 MINUTES
TOTAL TIME: 1 HOUR AND 45 MINUTES

This one may be "Old Fashioned," but for comfort food, it can't be beat.

INGREDIENTS

For the Dumplings

4 slices of bread, chopped

½ cup parsley, leaves removed and chopped

1¼ cup all-purpose flour

1 teaspoon baking powder

½ cup milk

1 egg

¼ cup unsalted butter, melted

1 cup cooked chicken leg meat, chopped

Salt and pepper, to taste

For the Chicken Broth

1 tablespoon vegetable oil

½ onion, finely chopped

1 carrot, peeled and finely chopped

1 celery stalk, finely chopped

1 sprig thyme, leaves removed and chopped

4 cups chicken stock (see page 14)

Salt and pepper, to taste

Parsley, chopped, for garnish

1 To make the Dumplings, place the bread and parsley in a food processor and pulse until combined. Add the flour and the baking powder, pulse, then slowly add the milk, egg, and butter. Pulse until a smooth paste forms and transfer to a mixing bowl. Fold in the chopped chicken meat and season with salt and pepper. Refrigerate for 1 hour.

2 Add the oil to a medium saucepan and warm over medium heat. Add the onions and cook for 5 minutes, or until soft. Add the remaining vegetables and cook until tender.

3 Add the thyme and the chicken stock and bring to a boil. Reduce the heat so that the soup simmers and cook for 20 minutes.

4 Drop tablespoon-sized balls of the chicken mixture into the simmering soup. Cover and cook for 12 minutes. Season with salt and pepper, ladle into bowls, and garnish with parsley.

Pork and Crab Wonton Soup

YIELD: 4 SERVINGS • ACTIVE TIME: 15 MINUTES • TOTAL TIME: 40 MINUTES

This quick and refreshing soup can work as an appetizer or a main course. The sweetness in this dish is balanced by the spiciness of the radish.

INGREDIENTS

For the Soup

1 tablespoon sesame oil

1 onion, diced

2 carrots, peeled and diced

2 garlic cloves, diced

1 cup mirin

4 cups crab stock (see page 17)

1 lemongrass stalk, bruised with the back of a knife

1 tablespoon soy sauce

1 tablespoon fish sauce

Salt and pepper, to taste

Sesame seeds, toasted, for garnish

Cilantro, chopped, for garnish

Sesame oil, for garnish

1 sheet of nori, broken, for garnish

For the Pork and Crab Wontons

4 oz. crab meat, cleaned, cooked, and diced

4 oz. ground pork

1 tablespoon shallots, minced

1 tablespoon chives, chopped

1 tablespoon fish sauce

2 tablespoons miso

2 tablespoons radish, chopped

1 tablespoon sesame seeds, toasted

1 teaspoon sesame oil

1 teaspoon sherry

12 wonton wrappers

1 In a medium saucepan, add the sesame oil and cook over medium heat until warm. Add the onion and carrots and cook for 5 minutes, or until soft.

2 Add the garlic and cook for 2 minutes. Add mirin, crab stock, lemongrass, soy sauce, and fish sauce. Simmer for 10 minutes, and then remove the lemongrass. Season with salt and pepper.

3 To make the wontons, place all ingredients in a bowl, save the wrappers, and mix until well combined.

4 Place 2 teaspoons of the mixture in the center of a wrapper. Dip a finger into cold water and rub around the entire edge of the wonton. Bring each corner of the wrapper together and seal it shut. Repeat with the remaining wrappers.

5 Bring the soup to a boil and add the wontons. Reduce heat so that the soup simmers and cook for 5 minutes, or until the wontons float to the top.

6 Place 3 wontons in each bowl, pour the soup over the wantons, and garnish with toasted sesame seeds, cilantro, sesame oil, and the broken nori.

Pot Sticker Broth

This very simple and flavorful broth will work well with either pork or shrimp pot stickers, whatever your preference.

INGREDIENTS

For the Pot Stickers

6 oz. ground pork or shrimp

½ cup cabbage, diced

1 tablespoon ginger, minced

4 scallions, sliced, whites and greens separated

1 tablespoon soy sauce

4 tablespoons water

24 wonton wrappers

1 egg, beaten

2 tablespoons oil

For the Broth

6 cups chicken stock (see page 14)

3 cups savoy cabbage, thinly sliced

2 cups shiitake mushroom caps, sliced

1 carrot, peeled and cut into matchsticks

½ cup peas

2 tablespoons soy sauce

Salt and pepper, to taste

Scallion greens, for garnish

Sesame oil, for garnish

1 To make the pot stickers, add the pork or shrimp to a bowl. Add the cabbage, ginger, scallion whites, soy sauce, and 2 tablespoons of the water and stir until combined.

2 Lay 6 wrappers on a clean, dry work surface. Dip a finger into the egg and rub it over the edge of each wonton wrapper.

3 Place a teaspoon of the filling in the middle of each wrapper. Fold over wrapper and seal by pinching the edges together. Repeat with the remaining wrappers.

4 Once complete, warm a large sauté pan over medium-high heat. Add the oil and warm for 1 minute. Add the pot stickers and cook for 2 minutes, or until nicely browned. Add the remaining water to the pan, cover, and cook for 3 minutes. Remove and place in serving bowls or refrigerate if using later.

5 For the broth, add the chicken stock to a medium saucepan and bring to a boil. Add the cabbage, mushrooms, and carrot, and cook for 3 minutes.

6 Add the peas and cook for 2 minutes. Add the soy sauce, and then season with salt and pepper. Ladle over pot stickers and garnish with scallion greens and sesame oil.

Simple Dumpling Soup

YIELD: 4 SERVINGS • ACTIVE TIME: 20 MINUTES • TOTAL TIME: 45 MINUTES

This is a very simple, yet satisfying soup. Feel free to add additional vegetables and/or beans if you want to make it heartier.

INGREDIENTS

For the Dumplings

1 cup all-purpose flour

½ teaspoon baking powder

½ teaspoon salt

½ tablespoon extra virgin olive oil

1 egg

6 tablespoons water

1 tablespoon chives, chopped

For the Soup

2 tablespoons unsalted butter

4 slices thick-cut bacon, chopped

1 onion, chopped

4 cups potato, peeled and chopped

6 cups chicken stock (see page 14)

Salt and pepper, to taste

1 To make the Dumplings, add the flour, baking powder, and salt to a mixing bowl and stir until combined.

2 Add the oil, egg, water, and chives and stir with a fork until a loose dough forms. Cover dough and set aside.

3 For the soup, add the butter to a medium saucepan and cook over medium heat until warm. Add the bacon and onion and cook for 5 minutes, or until the bacon is crispy and the onion is soft.

4 Add the potato and cook for 3 minutes. Add the stock and bring to a boil. Reduce heat so that the soup simmers and cook for 10 minutes, or until the potatoes are tender.

5 Season with salt and pepper. Drop tablespoon-sized dumplings into the broth. Once all of the dumplings have been incorporated, simmer for 3 minutes, then turn off the heat.

6 Let stand a few minutes, then ladle into warmed bowls and serve.

Szechuan-Spiced Shoyu Ramen

YIELD: 4 SERVINGS • ACTIVE TIME: 30 MINUTES • TOTAL TIME: 1 HOUR

This dish has a great aroma and spiciness. The ramen noodles cook very quickly, so make sure to have them ready by the time you prepare the poached eggs.

INGREDIENTS

For the Szechuan Peppercorn and Chili Oil

1½ cups vegetable oil

5 star anise

1 cinnamon stick

2 bay leaves

3 tablespoons Szechuan peppercorns

⅓ cup red pepper flakes

1 teaspoon salt

For the Crispy Scallions

1 cup oil

4 scallions, white part cut into thick matchsticks, greens reserved for garnish

Salt and pepper, to taste

For the Shoyu Ramen

2 tablespoons sesame oil

4 garlic cloves, minced

3-inch piece of ginger, minced

2 tablespoons chili bean sauce

3 cups chicken stock (see page 14)

3 cups dashi stock (see page 18)

¼ cup soy sauce

1 tablespoon sake

2 teaspoons sugar

Salt and pepper, to taste

Noodles from 2 packets of ramen

4 Poached Eggs, for garnish (see next page)

1 Start by preparing the Szechuan Peppercorn and Chili Oil. In a small saucepan, add the vegetable oil, star anise, cinnamon stick, bay leaves, and Szechuan peppercorns. Cook over the lowest-possible heat for 20 minutes, being careful not to burn.

2 Place the red pepper flakes in a small bowl. Strain the warm oil over the flakes. Let cool, season with salt, and reserve until ready to use.

3 To make the Crispy Scallions, place the oil in a Dutch oven and cook over medium-high heat until it reaches 350°F. Bring a pot of water to boil. Add the scallion whites and cook for 2 minutes. Remove, submerge in ice water, and then dry thoroughly.

4 Place the scallion whites into the oil. Stir constantly and fry until golden brown. Remove with a slotted spoon or large tweezers. Set on paper towels to drain, season with salt and pepper, and set aside.

5 To make the Shoyu Ramen, in a medium saucepan, add the sesame oil to a medium saucepan and warm over medium heat. Add the garlic and ginger and cook for 3 minutes, or until fragrant. Add the chili bean sauce and cook for 1 minute.

6 Add the chicken stock, dashi stock, soy sauce, and sake. Bring to a boil and then reduce to a simmer. Cook for 5 minutes, adjust the seasoning with sugar, salt, and pepper and turn off the heat.

7 Cook the noodles per manufacturer's instructions and serve in warm bowls. Bring the broth to a boil and then pour over the ramen noodles. Garnish with Poached Eggs, Szechuan Peppercorn and Chili Oil, Crispy Scallions, and scallion greens.

POACHED EGGS:

CRACK EACH EGG INTO A SMALL, INDIVIDUAL BOWL. IN A MEDIUM SAUCEPAN, ADD 3 CUPS WATER AND 2 TABLESPOONS WHITE VINEGAR AND BRING TO A BOIL. REDUCE TO A SIMMER AND GENTLY ADD THE EGGS ONE AT A TIME. COOK FOR 3 MINUTES, BASTING THE EGGS WITH THE POACHING WATER. REMOVE WITH A SLOTTED SPOON, PLACE ON PAPER TOWEL TO DRY, SEASON WITH SALT AND PEPPER, AND SERVE.

Vegetarian Ramen

YIELD: 4 SERVINGS • ACTIVE TIME: 15 MINUTES • TOTAL TIME: 45 MINUTES

This is a great vegetarian ramen, which gets its spice from the chili bean paste. If you want to make this a bit heartier, add a hardboiled or poached egg.

INGREDIENTS

For the Vegetarian Dashi Stock

3 cups water

1 oz. kombu

4 dried shiitake mushrooms

For the Ramen

2 tablespoons sesame oil

4 garlic cloves, minced

2-inch piece of ginger, minced

4 scallions, sliced, greens reserved for garnish

2 tablespoons chili bean paste

2 tablespoons miso

¼ cup sake

4 tablespoons black-and-white sesame seeds, toasted and ground into a paste, plus more for garnish

3 cups unsweetened soy milk

Salt and pepper, to taste

Noodles from 2 packages of ramen

Bean sprouts, for garnish

1 To make the stock, add the water and the kombu to in a heavy saucepan. Soak for 20 minutes. Remove the kombu and score the surface gently with a knife.

2 Return the kombu to the water and bring to a boil. Remove the kombu immediately, so that the broth doesn't become bitter. Add the dried shiitakes and return to a boil. Turn off heat and let stand until cool. Pass the stock through a fine sieve and refrigerate until ready to use.

3 To make the Ramen, add the sesame oil and cook over medium heat until warm. Add the garlic and ginger, and cook for 3 minutes, or until fragrant.

4 Add the scallions, chili bean paste, and miso, and cook for 1 minute. Add the sake and cook until half of it has evaporated.

5 Add the sesame seed paste, 2 cups stock, and soy milk, and bring to a boil. Season with salt and pepper, and remove pan from heat.

6 Cook the noodles per manufacturer's instructions. Place the noodles into warm bowls and pour the broth over them. Garnish with scallion greens, toasted sesame seeds, and bean sprouts.

Avgolemono with Orzo Salad

YIELD: 4 SERVINGS • ACTIVE TIME: 45 MINUTES • TOTAL TIME: 1 HOUR

One of the most popular soups in Greek cuisine, "avgolemono" means egg and lemon, which combine here to produce a nourishing soup that is still nice and light.

1 Pour the stock into a large saucepan and bring to a boil. Reduce the heat so that the broth simmers. Add the chicken thighs and cook for 20 minutes.

2 Remove the chicken thighs and set aside. Add the orzo and cook for 5 minutes. Meanwhile, remove the meat from the chicken thighs, discard the skin and bones, and chop the meat into bite-sized pieces.

3 Strain the orzo from the broth and set aside. Return the broth to the pan and bring to a simmer.

4 In a mixing bowl, add the eggs and beat until frothy. Add the lemon juice and cold water and whisk. Add approximately $1/2$ cup of the stock to bowl and stir constantly.

5 Add another cup of hot stock to the egg mixture and then add the contents of the bowl to the saucepan. Be careful not to let the stock boil once you add the egg mixture, otherwise it will curdle.

6 Add half of the cooked orzo and the chicken to the saucepan. Season with salt and pepper and ladle into warmed bowls. Garnish with parsley and lemon slices and set aside.

7 To make the Orzo Salad, add the orzo, feta cheese, bell peppers, Kalamata olives, scallions, capers, garlic, parsley, and pine nuts to a medium sized mixing bowl and stir until combined.

8 In a small bowl, add the lemon juice, vinegar, mustard, and cumin and stir until combined. Gradually whisk in the olive oil and then add the dressing to the orzo mixture. Toss to blend, season with salt and pepper, cover, and refrigerate until ready to serve.

INGREDIENTS

For the Avgolemono

6 cups chicken stock
(see page 14)

2 chicken thighs

1 cup orzo pasta

3 eggs

1 tablespoon lemon juice

1 tablespoon cold water

Salt and pepper, to taste

Parsley, chopped,
for garnish

Lemon slices, for garnish

For the Orzo Salad

½ cup of orzo, cooked

¼ cup feta cheese,
crumbled

¼ cup red bell pepper, chopped

3 tablespoons yellow bell pepper,
chopped

3 tablespoons Kalamata olives,
chopped

1 scallion, sliced

1 teaspoon capers,
drained and chopped

1 teaspoon garlic, minced

1 teaspoon parsley, leaves
removed and chopped

1 tablespoon pine nuts,
toasted and chopped

2 teaspoons lemon juice

1 teaspoon white
wine vinegar

1 teaspoon Dijon mustard

½ teaspoon cumin

3 tablespoons extra virgin olive oil

Salt and pepper, to taste

Coconut and Spinach Soup with Toasted Sliced Almonds

YIELD: 4 SERVINGS • ACTIVE TIME: 20 MINUTES • TOTAL TIME: 45 MINUTES

Coconut and spinach are not usually two flavors that people pair together, but once you try this soup you'll wonder why no one thought of it sooner.

INGREDIENTS

3 tablespoons unsalted butter

1 onion, chopped

16 cups spinach, chopped

4 cups vegetable stock (see page 25)

1 tablespoon all-purpose flour

2 cups coconut milk

Salt and pepper, to taste

¼ teaspoon nutmeg, plus more for garnish

Chives, chopped, for garnish

Almonds, sliced and toasted, for garnish

Unsweetened shredded coconut, for garnish

1 Place 2 tablespoons of the butter in a medium saucepan and cook over medium heat until melted. Add the onion and cook for 5 minutes, or until soft.

2 Add the spinach, cover, and cook over low heat for 5 minutes, or until wilted. Add the stock and bring to a boil. Transfer the soup to a food processor, blend until creamy, and strain through a fine sieve.

3 In a clean medium saucepan, add the remaining butter and melt. Add the flour and cook for 2 minutes. Add the soup and coconut milk to the pan with the butter and flour. Cook for 5 minutes. Season with salt, pepper, and nutmeg, ladle into warm bowls, and garnish with nutmeg, chives, almonds, and coconut.

Tomato Soup with Chickpeas and Pasta

YIELD: 4 SERVINGS • ACTIVE TIME: 20 MINUTES • TOTAL TIME: 45 MINUTES

The canned tomatoes help provide consistent flavor year-round in this filling, healthy soup.

INGREDIENTS

2 tablespoons extra virgin olive oil

1 onion, chopped

2 garlic cloves, minced

4 (14 oz.) cans stewed tomatoes, pureed

2 thyme sprigs, leaves removed and chopped

4 cups chicken stock (see page 14)

½ cup ditalini pasta

1 (14 oz.) can chickpeas, rinsed and drained

¼ cup parsley, leaves removed and chopped

¼ cup Parmesan cheese, grated, plus more for garnish

Salt and pepper, to taste

Basil, chopped, for garnish

1 In a large saucepan, add the oil and cook over medium heat until warm. Add the onion and cook for 5 minutes, or until soft. Add the garlic and cook for 2 minutes. Then, add the pureed tomatoes, thyme, and stock and bring to a boil.

2 Reduce heat so that the soup simmers. Add the ditalini pasta and cook for 8 to 10 minutes, or until the pasta is tender.

3 Add the chickpeas, parsley, and Parmesan and cook for 3 minutes. Season with salt and pepper and serve in warm bowls garnished with Parmesan cheese and basil.

Vegetables, Legumes, Nuts, and Grains

Vegetables allow you to experience one the best things about soup: how easily it can follow the changing seasons. Vegetable soups are also a great way to showcase a vegetable that is no longer at its prettiest, as this extra bit of ripening converts the carbohydrates to natural sugars and gives the soup even more flavor.

Unlike many meat-centric soups, vegetable soups do not typically need a lot of time to develop their flavors—they have them naturally.

Legumes, grains, and nuts add a great deal of nutrition, texture, and flavor to these recipes. In some soups, they provide the main flavor profile, and in others they play a supporting role. This is part of the magic of these ingredients—they are versatile and capable of whatever task is assigned to them.

It's worth noting that if a recipe requires dried beans, the beans need to soak overnight. Soaking the beans cleans them, removes some of their natural sugars, and softens them, which will decrease the cooking time. The reduction in cooking time is most important, as it will prevent you from overcooking and throwing the entire dish out of balance. So, when using dried beans, make sure you start your preparations the night before.

Chili Tortilla Soup

Tortilla soup is one of Mexico's best-known soups, and with all the options available, it's easy to see why.

1 Preheat oven to 350°F. Place the garlic in an ungreased, nonstick pan. Cook over medium heat for 15 minutes, or until blackened, turning occasionally. Remove the garlic from the pan and allow to cool. When cool, peel and mince.

2 Place the tomato on a baking tray. Place the tray in the oven and cook for 10 minutes. Remove and set aside, making sure to save any juices.

3 In a medium saucepan, add 1 tablespoon of vegetable oil and warm over low heat. Add the onion and cook for 10 minutes, or until golden brown.

4 Place the rehydrated chilies in a food processor with the roasted garlic, tomato, the tomato's juices, and 1 cup of stock. Puree until smooth, strain though a fine sieve, and add to the cooked onions and salt. Add the remaining stock and simmer for 30 minutes.

5 Meanwhile, place the remaining 2 cups of oil in a Dutch oven and warm to 350°F. Place the tortilla strips into the oil and fry, turning frequently until crisp. Remove with a slotted spoon and set on paper towels to drain.

6 After 30 minutes, add the red Swiss chard to the soup and cook for 5 minutes. Ladle into bowls and serve with the tortilla strips, Monterey Jack cheese, and limes.

INGREDIENTS

2 garlic cloves, unpeeled

1 tomato

2 cups vegetable oil, plus
1 tablespoon

1 onion, sliced

1½ oz. dried pasilla
chilies, stemmed,
seeded, and soaked in
hot water for
20 minutes, then drained

6 cups chicken stock
(see page 14)

½ teaspoon salt

8 corn tortillas, cut into
¼-inch strips

4 cups red Swiss chard,
thinly sliced

2 cups Monterey Jack
cheese, grated, for
garnish

1 small lime, cut into
quarters, for garnish

Broccoli and Cheddar Soup with Parmesan Crisps

YIELD: 4 SERVINGS • ACTIVE TIME: 15 MINUTES • TOTAL TIME: 30 MINUTES

This very simple and quick soup is sure to become a family favorite. Cauliflower can be used as a variation.

INGREDIENTS

For the Broccoli and Cheddar Soup

2 tablespoons extra virgin olive oil

1 onion, chopped

¼ cup unsalted butter

¼ cup all-purpose flour

2 cups milk

2 cups chicken stock (see page 14)

1½ cups broccoli florets

1 cup carrots, peeled and cut into matchsticks

2 celery stalks, sliced

2 cups sharp cheddar cheese, grated

Salt and pepper, to taste

For the Parmesan Crisps

1 cup Parmesan cheese, grated

1 cup sharp cheddar cheese, grated

Cayenne pepper, to taste

1 To prepare the soup, add the oil to a medium saucepan and warm over medium heat. Add the onion and cook for 5 minutes, or until soft.

2 Add the butter. When the butter is melted, slowly add the flour, while stirring constantly. Cook for 3 minutes, and then add the milk and chicken stock.

3 Bring to a boil, reduce heat so that the soup simmers, and add the broccoli florets, carrots, and celery. Cook for 8 minutes, or until vegetables are cooked through. Add cheddar cheese and mix until combined. Season with salt and pepper, and keep warm while you prepare the Parmesan Crisps.

4 To make the crisps, preheat oven to 400°F. In a mixing bowl, add the cheeses and mix until combined. Sprinkle the cheese on a lined baking tray. Make 8 circles, using a ring cutter to help keep them round.

5 Place a pinch of cayenne on each crisp. Place the tray in the oven and cook for 7 minutes, or until melted.

Caramelized Onion Soup with Baked Herbed Croutons

YIELD: 4 SERVINGS • ACTIVE TIME: 30 MINUTES • TOTAL TIME: 1 HOUR

Caramelizing the onions allows for the natural sugars to concentrate and make the onions nice and sweet. Combining them with the Madeira is sure to make everyone happy.

INGREDIENTS

For the Caramelized Onion Soup

¼ cup unsalted butter

6 Spanish onions, chopped

2 garlic cloves, minced

1 sprig thyme, leaves removed and chopped

½ cup Riesling

½ cup Madeira

4 cups heavy cream

Salt and pepper, to taste

For the Baked Herb Croutons

1 tablespoon parsley, chopped

1 tablespoon tarragon, chopped

1 tablespoon chives, chopped

¼ cup extra virgin olive oil

8 slices of French bread

Salt and pepper, to taste

1 In a medium saucepan, add the butter and cook over low heat until melted. Add the onions and cook over the lowest possible heat for 30 minutes, or until golden brown. Stir the onions every few minutes and add small amounts of water when they begin to stick to the pan.

2 Add the garlic, thyme, Riesling, and Madeira and cook until the liquid has been reduced by half. Add the cream, salt, and pepper and simmer for 10 minutes.

3 While the soup is simmering, start the croutons by preheating the oven to 350°F. Combine the herbs and olive oil in a small bowl. Place slices of baguette on a baking tray and drizzle with the herbed olive oil.

4 Season with salt and pepper, place in the oven, and bake for 10 minutes until golden brown. Allow to cool.

5 Once the soup has finished simmering, transfer it to a food processor and blend until smooth. Season to taste with salt and pepper and serve with Baked Herbed Croutons.

Carrot and Ginger Soup with Turmeric Cream

YIELD: 4 TO 6 SERVINGS • ACTIVE TIME: 25 MINUTES • TOTAL TIME: 1 HOUR

This soup is for the true ginger lover, or for when you feel a cold coming on.

INGREDIENTS

For the Carrot and Ginger Soup

4 tablespoons unsalted butter

2 onions, diced

6 cups carrots, peeled and chopped

4 tablespoons ginger, peeled and minced

Zest and juice of 2 oranges

1 cup white wine

8 cups chicken stock (see page 14) or vegetable stock (see page 25)

Salt and pepper, to taste

Dill, chopped, for garnish

For the Turmeric Cream

½ cup heavy cream

½ teaspoon turmeric

Pinch of salt

1 In a medium saucepan, add the butter and cook over medium heat until melted. Add the onions and cook for 5 minutes, while stirring often, or until soft.

2 Add the carrots, ginger, and orange zest. Cook for 5 minutes, or until the carrot starts to break down.

3 Add the orange juice and white wine and cook until evaporated. Add the stock, bring to a boil, and season with salt and pepper. Reduce heat so that the soup simmers and cook for 10 to 15 minutes, until the vegetables are tender.

4 Transfer the soup to a food processor, puree until smooth, and strain through a fine sieve. Return the soup to a clean pan and adjust the seasoning. Add more stock or juice if it is too thick.

5 To make the Tumeric Cream, place the cream in a bowl and whip until medium peaks begin to form. Add the tumeric and season with salt. Stir to combine. Ladle into warm bowls, serve with Turmeric Cream, and garnish with dill.

Chilled Sweet and Sour Beet Soup

YIELD: 4 SERVINGS • ACTIVE TIME: 20 MINUTES • TOTAL TIME: 2 HOURS

This is a summer classic. You can even add vodka and serve it as a shooter.

INGREDIENTS

2 tablespoons unsalted butter

2 tablespoons vegetable oil

1 red onion, chopped

6 cups beets, peeled and chopped

2 celery stalks, chopped

1 red bell pepper, seeded and chopped

2 small apples, peeled and chopped

6 cups vegetable stock (see page 25)

1 teaspoon cumin

1 teaspoon thyme, leaves removed and chopped

2 bay leaves

½ cup sour cream, plus more for garnish

½ cup heavy cream

2 teaspoons lemon juice

Salt and pepper, to taste

Dill, for garnish

1 In a large saucepan, add the butter and oil and cook over medium heat until warm. Add the onion, beets, celery, red bell pepper, and apples and cook for 5 minutes, or until the onion is soft.

2 Add the stock, cumin, thyme, and bay leaves and bring to a boil. Reduce heat so that the soup simmers and cook for 30 minutes, or until the vegetables are soft.

3 Transfer the soup to a food processor, puree until creamy, and strain through a fine sieve.

4 Return to a clean pan, add sour cream, heavy cream, and lemon juice and bring to a simmer. Season with salt and pepper, place in the refrigerator, and chill for 1 hour. Serve in chilled bowls and garnish with sour cream and dill.

Corn Chowder with Corn Beignets

YIELD: 4 TO 6 SERVINGS • ACTIVE TIME: 25 MINUTES
TOTAL TIME: 2 HOURS AND 15 MINUTES

There is nothing better than fresh corn from your local farm stand, and turning it into a soup is a great way to show off its lovely characteristics. For a more rustic version, skip the food processor.

INGREDIENTS

For the Corn Chowder

6 ears of corn, kernels removed, cobs reserved

4 oz. bacon, chopped

1 large white onion, chopped

3 garlic cloves, minced

2 large potatoes, peeled and chopped

4 cups heavy cream

Salt and pepper, to taste

For the Corn Beignets

¼ cup milk

⅛ teaspoon salt

2 tablespoons unsalted butter

¼ cup all-purpose cup flour

1 egg

¼ cup corn

½ teaspoon cilantro, chopped

2 cups olive oil

1 In a stockpot, place the reserved cobs and cover with water. Bring to a boil, reduce heat so that the stock simmers, and cook for 1 hour. Strain the stock, measure out 4 cups, and reserve.

2 In a large saucepan, add the bacon and cook over medium heat until fat renders. Add the onion and garlic and cook for 5 minutes or until soft.

3 Add the potatoes and corn kernels and cook for another 10 minutes, while stirring occasionally. Add the corn stock and cook until reduced by a third. Add the cream and simmer for 30 minutes

4 While the soup simmers, start on the Corn Beignets. In a medium saucepan, add milk, salt, and butter and bring to a boil. Add the flour and stir constantly until a ball of dough forms. Remove the pan from heat and let the dough cool for 10 minutes.

5 Add the egg to the pan and whisk vigorously. Once the egg has been combined, add the corn and cilantro and stir until combined.

6 Place the oil in a Dutch oven and heat to 350°F. Spoon small amounts of the batter into the hot oil and cook until golden brown. Remove with a slotted spoon and set on a paper towel to drain.

7 Season the soup with salt and pepper, ladle into warm bowls, and serve with Corn Beignets.

Artichoke Soup with Fennel Seed Yogurt

YIELD: 4 SERVINGS • ACTIVE TIME: 20 MINUTES • TOTAL TIME: 45 MINUTES

Artichokes are a vegetable that people often shy away from. So why not try them in a soup? After peeling and cleaning the artichokes, place them in lemon water to prevent oxidation.

INGREDIENTS

For the Fennel Seed Yogurt

1 teaspoon ground fennel seed

1 cup Greek yogurt

2 tablespoons Pernod

For the Artichoke Soup

1 tablespoon vegetable oil

1 tablespoon unsalted butter

6 artichokes, peeled and hearts sliced thin

1 garlic clove, minced

1 onion, diced

1 cup Riesling

1 sprig thyme, leaves removed and chopped

4 cups heavy cream

1 cup vegetable stock

Salt and pepper, to taste

Dill, chopped, for garnish

1 Start by making the Fennel Seed Yogurt. For a stronger flavor, roast and cool the fennel seeds before grinding them. Combine all ingredients in a bowl. Place in refrigerator and chill until ready to use.

2 To make the soup, place the oil and butter in a medium saucepan. Add the artichokes, garlic, and onion and cook over medium heat for 10 minutes.

3 Add the Riesling and thyme and cook until the wine has been reduced by half. Add the heavy cream and the vegetable stock and simmer for 10 minutes.

4 Transfer the soup to a food processor, puree until smooth, and strain through a fine sieve. Season to taste with salt and pepper, ladle into warm bowls, serve with the Fennel Seed Yogurt, and garnish with dill.

French Onion Soup

YIELD: 4 SERVINGS • ACTIVE TIME: 30 MINUTES
TOTAL TIME: 1 HOUR AND 15 MINUTES

Should you only make one recipe from this book, let it be this one. You'll be hard pressed to find someone who dislikes this soup.

INGREDIENTS

5 onions, 1 halved, the remaining 4 sliced very thin

2 tablespoons vegetable oil

½ cup sherry

1 tablespoon Worcestershire sauce

2 teaspoons thyme, chopped

8 cups chicken stock (see page 14)

Salt and pepper, to taste

4 slices of sourdough bread

1½ cups Gruyère cheese, grated

1 Place the halved onion over an open flame and char. Set aside.

2 Place the oil in a medium saucepan. Add the remaining onions and cook on the lowest heat setting for 30 minutes or until golden brown. Stir the onions every few minutes and add small amounts of water when the onions begin to stick.

3 Deglaze the pan with the sherry and Worcestershire sauce. Cook until liquid has been reduced by half. Add the thyme, stock, and the charred onion half and cook until reduced by half.

4 Meanwhile, preheat your oven to its broiler setting. Remove the charred onion, season the soup with salt and pepper, pour into ceramic bowls, and cover with a slice of sourdough bread and cheese. Place the bowls on the oven's top rack, cook until the cheese has melted, and serve.

Irish Leek and Cashel Blue Cheese Soup with Blue Cheese Fritters

YIELD: 6 SERVINGS • ACTIVE TIME: 30 MINUTES • TOTAL TIME: 1 HOUR

If you like blue cheese and haven't tried Cashel blue cheese, remedy that immediately. If you have, you know that it is perfect for this traditional Irish soup.

INGREDIENTS

For the Blue Cheese Fritters

2 cups oil

3 eggs

¼ cup all-purpose flour

1 cup panko bread crumbs, reduced to a fine powder in a food processor

6 oz. Cashel Blue, rolled into 12 balls or cut into 12 cubes

Salt, to taste

For the Irish Leek and Cashel Blue Cheese Soup

¼ cup unsalted butter

2 tablespoons vegetable oil

3 large leeks, thinly sliced

8 oz. Cashel blue cheese

2 tablespoons all-purpose flour

1 tablespoon whole grain mustard, plus more for garnish

6 cups chicken stock (see page 14)

Black pepper, to taste

Chives, chopped, for garnish

1 To make the Blue Cheese Fritters, place the oil in a medium saucepan and heat to 350°F. Place the eggs in a bowl and beat with a fork. Place the flour and bread crumbs in separate bowls.

2 Dredge the cheese in the flour, remove, and shake to remove any excess flour. Place the floured blue cheese in the egg wash and coat evenly. Remove from egg wash, shake to remove any excess egg, and gently coat with bread crumbs. Repeat with the egg wash and bread crumbs until the cheese has been used up.

3 Place the cheese in the hot oil and fry until golden brown. Use a slotted spoon to remove the fritters from the oil, set on paper towels to drain, and season with salt.

4 To make the soup, add the butter and oil to a medium saucepan and warm over low heat. Add the leeks and gently cook for 5 minutes, or until softened.

5 Break the Cashel blue cheese into small pieces and add to the saucepan. Cook, while stirring, until the cheese is melted.

6 Add the flour and cook for 2 minutes, while stirring constantly, then season to taste with the mustard.

7 Slowly add the stock, stirring to prevent any lumps from forming. Bring to a boil, reduce heat so that the soup simmers, and cook for 10 minutes.

8 Season with pepper and ladle into warm bowls. Garnish with chives and mustard and serve with the Blue Cheese Fritters.

Miso Broth with Fried Tofu

YIELD: 4 SERVINGS • ACTIVE TIME: 30 MINUTES • TOTAL TIME: 1 HOUR

Try using Azuki Bean Miso from South River Miso, in Conway, Massachusetts for this recipe. If you have yet to try their miso, you certainly should. They are a family-run company and their products are outstanding.

INGREDIENTS

For the Fried Tofu

2 cups vegetable oil

2 eggs, whisked together

¼ cup all-purpose flour

1½ cups panko bread crumbs, ground to a fine powder in a food processor

5 oz. tofu, cut into ¾-inch cubes, dried on a paper towel

Salt, to taste

For the Crispy Wonton Skins

4 wonton wrappers, cut into triangles

Salt, to taste

For the Miso Broth

4 scallions, whites sliced thin, greens reserved for broth

4 cilantro sprigs, leaves reserved for garnish, stalks reserved for broth

1-inch piece ginger, sliced

1 star anise

1 cinnamon stick

4 cardamom pods, seeds removed from shell and crushed

1 bay leaf

½ teaspoon red pepper flakes

4 cups dashi stock (see page 18)

3 bok choy, cut lengthwise into eighths

¼ cup red miso

2 tablespoons soy sauce

Thai chili, seeds removed, thinly sliced, for garnish

1 Start by making the Fried Tofu. Place the oil in a medium saucepan and heat to 350°F. Place the eggs, flour, and panko bread crumbs in 3 separate bowls.

2 Dredge the tofu in the flour, remove, and shake to remove any excess flour. Place the coated tofu in the egg wash. Remove from egg wash, shake to release any excess egg, and gently coat with bread crumbs. If there is any tofu exposed, return to the egg mix and repeat with bread crumbs.

3 Once all the tofu is coated, place in oil and fry in batches until golden brown. Remove with a slotted spoon, place on a paper towel, and season with salt.

4 To make the Crispy Wonton Skins, place the wonton wrappers in the reserved oil and turn frequently until they are crisp and golden brown. Use a slotted spoon to remove the fried wonton wrappers from oil, set on paper towels to drain, and season with salt.

5 For the Miso Broth, add the scallion greens, cilantro stalks, ginger, star anise, cinnamon stick, cardamom seeds, bay leaf, red pepper flakes, and dashi stock to a stockpot. Cook over medium heat until boiling, reduce the heat, and simmer for 10 minutes.

6 Strain the broth through a fine sieve. Return to the stockpot and bring to a simmer.

7 Add the bok choy and cook for 5 minutes. Add the scallion whites and cook for an additional 2 minutes.Place the miso in a small bowl, add a bit of the hot stock, and then place in the soup.

8 Add soy sauce. Ladle into warm bowls, garnish with the cilantro and Thai chili, and serve with Fried Tofu and Crispy Wonton Skins.

Sweet Potato Soup

YIELD: 4 TO 6 SERVINGS • ACTIVE TIME: 25 MINUTES • TOTAL TIME: 1 HOUR

Do you love sweet potatoes? Then you are certain to love this soup. The curry is very subtle, but it adds a nice bit of flavor.

INGREDIENTS

For the Sweet Potato Soup

1½ tablespoons unsalted butter

1 small onion, chopped

5 cups chicken stock (see page 14)

½ teaspoon curry powder, plus more for garnish

10 cups sweet potatoes, peeled and chopped

2 tablespoons maple syrup

2 sprigs thyme, leaves removed and chopped

Pinch of cayenne pepper

2 cups heavy cream

2 pinches of ground nutmeg

Salt and pepper, to taste

Cilantro, for garnish

For the Rum Cream

½ cup heavy cream

¼ teaspoon lemon juice

⅛ teaspoon lemon zest

2 tablespoons Myers's Rum

Pinch of sugar

1 In a medium saucepan, add the butter and cook over medium heat until melted. Add the onion and cook for 5 minutes, or until soft.

2 Add the chicken stock, curry powder, sweet potato, maple syrup, thyme, and cayenne pepper. Bring to a boil, reduce heat so that the soup simmers, and cook for 25 minutes, or until the sweet potatoes are soft.

3 Remove the thyme sprigs and transfer the soup to a food processor. Puree until creamy and then pass through a fine sieve.

4 Return the soup to the pan and bring to a simmer. Add the cream, nutmeg, salt, and pepper.

5 To make the Rum Cream, add the cream to a bowl and whip until medium peaks form. Add the lemon juice, lemon zest, rum, and sugar. Stir to combine and set aside.

6 Ladle the soup into bowls and garnish with a dollop of Rum Cream, a sprinkle of curry powder, and cilantro.

Tomato and Basil Soup with Grissini

YIELD: 4 TO 6 SERVINGS • ACTIVE TIME: 45 MINUTES • TOTAL TIME: 1½ HOURS

Make sure your tomatoes are nice and ripe and, preferably, from your garden.

INGREDIENTS

For the Grissini

½ cup bread flour, plus 2 tablespoons

1 teaspoon salt

1½ teaspoons yeast

2½ tablespoons semolina flour

1½ teaspoons extra virgin olive oil

6 tablespoons warm water

1½ teaspoons dried parsley

1½ teaspoons oregano

1½ teaspoons poppy seeds

½ teaspoon caraway seeds

For the Tomato and Basil Soup

2 tablespoons extra virgin olive oil

2 tablespoons unsalted butter

1 onion, chopped

2 lbs. tomatoes, chopped

1 garlic clove, minced

3 cups vegetable stock (see page 25)

½ cup white wine

3 tablespoons tomato paste

Salt and pepper, to taste

½ cup basil, chopped, plus more for garnish

1 cup heavy cream

Romano cheese, grated, for garnish

1 To make the Grissini, preheat the oven to 375°F. Place the bread flour, salt, yeast, and semolina flour in a bowl and mix by hand until combined. Gradually add the oil and water and mix until well combined.

2 Add the herbs and seeds and combine. Place on a floured work surface and knead for 5 minutes. Place in a bowl, cover with a moist towel, and let stand for 20 minutes.

3 Cut the dough into 4 pieces. Cut the pieces into 6 strips. On a lightly floured work surface roll the strips out until they are 12 inches long. Place on a lined baking tray and let stand for 5 minutes.

4 Place in the oven and bake for 20 minutes, or until golden brown. Remove and let cool.

5 To make the soup, add the oil and butter to a medium saucepan and cook over medium heat until warm. Add the onion and cook for 5 minutes, or until soft.

6 Stir in the tomatoes and garlic, cook for 2 minutes, and then add the stock, white wine, and tomato paste. Bring to a boil, reduce to a simmer, season with salt and pepper, and cook for 20 minutes.

7 Transfer the soup to a food processor, add the basil, and puree until creamy. Strain through a fine sieve, return to a clean pan, add the heavy cream, and bring to a simmer.

8 Adjust seasoning to taste, ladle into warm bowls, garnish with a sprinkle of Romano cheese and basil, and serve with Grissini Sticks.

Vegetarian Green Gumbo

YIELD: 4 TO 6 SERVINGS • ACTIVE TIME: 30 MINUTES • TOTAL TIME: 45 MINUTES

This revitalizing and healthy gumbo will go great with a fresh baguette or toasted garlic bread.

INGREDIENTS

1 tablespoon vegetable oil

1 onion, chopped

2 garlic cloves, minced

1 celery stalk, diced

1 green bell pepper, chopped

¼ green cabbage, core removed and finely sliced

½ teaspoon oregano, leaves removed and chopped

½ teaspoon thyme, leaves removed and chopped

1 bay leaf

6 cups vegetable stock (see page 25)

2 cups collard greens, grated

2 cups spinach, grated

1 bunch watercress

12 oz. tofu, cut into ¼-inch pieces

¼ cup parsley, leaves removed and chopped

½ teaspoon allspice

Pinch of cayenne pepper

Salt and pepper, to taste

1 In a large saucepan, add the oil and cook over medium heat until warm. Add the onions, garlic, celery, and bell pepper and cook for 5 minutes, or until soft. Add the cabbage, oregano, thyme, and bay leaf and cook for 5 minutes.

2 Add the stock and bring to a boil. Reduce heat so that the soup simmers and cook for 5 minutes. Add the collard greens and cook for 5 minutes, then add the spinach, watercress, and tofu.

3 Cook for 2 minutes before adding the parsley, allspice, and cayenne. Season with salt and pepper, simmer for 2 minutes, and then serve in warm bowls.

Vegetables, Legumes, Nuts, and Grains

Sausage Barley Soup

YIELD: 4 SERVINGS • ACTIVE TIME: 20 MINUTES • TOTAL TIME: 1½ HOURS

This barley soup is very hearty and flavorful. It's also a great soup for the pressure cooker.

INGREDIENTS

2 tablespoons extra virgin olive oil

1 lb. ground Italian sausage

1 onion, diced

2 garlic cloves, minced

1 teaspoon basil, leaves removed and chopped

1 teaspoon oregano, leaves removed and chopped

1 teaspoon thyme, leaves removed and chopped

8 cups chicken stock (see page 14)

1 carrot, peeled and sliced

¼ cup pearl barley

10 oz. spinach, chopped

Salt and pepper, to taste

Focaccia or crusty bread, to serve

1 In a medium saucepan, add the olive oil and cook over medium-high heat until warm.

2 Add the sausage, onion, and garlic and cook for 5 minutes, using a wooden spoon to break up the sausage as it cooks. When the sausage is nicely browned, add the herbs and stock and bring to a boil.

3 Reduce heat so that the soup simmers and add the carrot and barley. Turn the heat down to its lowest setting and cover the saucepan. Cook for 1 hour, or until the barley is tender.

4 Add the spinach and cook for 5 minutes, or until wilted. Season with salt and pepper and serve in warm bowls with focaccia or crusty bread.

French Lentil Soup

YIELD: 4 TO 6 SERVINGS • ACTIVE TIME: 25 MINUTES
TOTAL TIME: 1 HOUR AND 15 MINUTES

This traditional French soup is sure to warm the bones.

1 To start the Caraway Water Biscuits, preheat oven to 350°F. Add the flour and water to a mixing bowl and whisk until combined. Add the salt.

2 On a parchment-lined baking tray, use a pastry brush to transfer the batter to the tray, taking care to make nice, long crackers.

3 Sprinkle with caraway seeds and place in the oven. Bake for 8 minutes, or until golden brown, then remove the tray and let crackers cool.

4 Begin the soup by adding oil to a medium saucepan. Warm over medium heat, then add the onion and garlic and cook for 5 minutes, or until the onion is soft. Add the carrot, leek, and celery, and cook for 5 minutes, or until soft. Add the tomato paste and cook, while stirring, for 2 minutes.

5 Add the lentils, stock, Sachet d'Epices, bay leaf, thyme, caraway seeds, and lemon slices. Bring to a boil, reduce heat so that the soup simmers, and cook for 30 minutes, or until the lentils are tender.

6 Remove the Sachet d'Epices and lemon slices. Add the vinegar and Riesling and season with salt and pepper. Serve in warmed bowls with Caraway Water Biscuits.

INGREDIENTS

For the Caraway Water Biscuits

½ cup all-purpose flour

10 tablespoons water

⅛ teaspoon salt

2 tablespoons caraway seeds

For the French Lentil Soup

2 tablespoons vegetable oil

1 onion, peeled and chopped

1 garlic clove, minced

1 carrot, peeled and minced

1 leek, white part only, minced

1 celery stalk, minced

1 tablespoon tomato paste

1½ cups French lentils

6 cups chicken stock (see page 14)

1 Sachet d'Epices (see sidebar)

1 bay leaf

2 sprigs thyme, leaves removed and chopped

¼ teaspoon caraway seeds

½ lemon, sliced

½ oz. apple cider vinegar

¼ cup Riesling

Salt and pepper, to taste

SACHET D'EPICES: CUT A 4-INCH SQUARE OF CHEESECLOTH AND A 12-INCH PIECE OF BUTCHER TWINE. PLACE 3 PARSLEY STEMS, ¼ TEASPOON THYME LEAVES, ½ BAY LEAF, ¼ TEASPOON. CRACKED PEPPERCORNS, AND ½ GARLIC CLOVE, MINCED, IN THE MIDDLE OF THE CHEESECLOTH AND LIFT EACH CORNER TO CREATE A PURSE. TIE ONE SIDE OF THE TWINE AROUND THE CORNERS AND MAKE A KNOT. TIE THE OTHER SIDE OF THE TWINE TO THE HANDLE OF YOUR POT AND THEN TOSS IN THE SACHET D'EPICE.

Moroccan Legume Soup with Honey Buns

YIELD: 4 SERVINGS • ACTIVE TIME: 45 MINUTES • TOTAL TIME: 13 HOURS

This very healthy, authentic Moroccan soup showcases all the flavors of North African cuisine.

INGREDIENTS

For the Honey Buns

½ teaspoon dried yeast

1 tablespoon lukewarm water

1¾ cups bread flour

½ teaspoon salt

2 tablespoons honey

1 teaspoon fennel seeds

1 cup milk, plus 1 tablespoon

1 egg yolk

1 teaspoon poppy seeds, optional

For the Moroccan Legume Soup

1½ tablespoons extra virgin olive oil

1 onion, peeled, halved, and sliced

¼ teaspoon ground ginger

¼ teaspoon turmeric

½ teaspoon cinnamon

⅛ teaspoon saffron threads

1 (14 oz.) can diced tomatoes

1 teaspoon sugar

½ cup chickpeas, soaked overnight and strained

4 cups veal stock (see page 12)

⅓ cup brown lentils, soaked overnight and strained

½ cup dried fava beans, soaked overnight and strained

1 tablespoon cilantro, leaves removed and chopped

1 tablespoon parsley, leaves removed and chopped

Salt and pepper, to taste

1 To make the Honey Buns, combine the yeast and lukewarm water in a bowl and let stand until yeast is dissolved.

2 Sieve the flour and salt into a mixing bowl. Add the dissolved yeast, honey, and fennel seeds, then slowly add 1 cup of the milk. Stir until well-combined.

3 Place the dough on a floured work surface and knead for 5 minutes, until it is smooth and elastic.

4 Cover the dough with a damp cloth and let stand until it has doubled in size.

5 Preheat the oven to 450°F. Divide the dough into 12 pieces and shape each piece into a ball. Place on a baking tray and let stand for 10 minutes.

6 Combine the egg yolk and 1 tablespoon of milk in a small bowl. Brush the top of each bun with the egg mixture, sprinkle on the poppy seeds, if using, and place in the oven. Bake for 15 minutes, or until golden brown on top and bottom.

7 Remove the buns from the tray and place on a wire rack to cool.

8 To begin the soup, In a medium saucepan, add the oil and cook over medium heat until warm. Add the onions and cook for 5 minutes, or until soft.

9 Add the ginger, turmeric, cinnamon, saffron threads, tomatoes, and sugar. Stir in the chickpeas and the stock and bring to a boil. Reduce heat so that the soup simmers, cover, and cook for 10 minutes.

10 Add the lentils and fava beans and continue to cook for 15 minutes, or until all the legumes are tender. Add the cilantro and parsley, season with salt and pepper, and serve in warmed bowls with Honey Buns.

Split Pea Soup with Smoked Ham

YIELD: 4 SERVINGS • ACTIVE TIME: 30 MINUTES • TOTAL TIME: 1½ TO 2 HOURS

This Greek soup is traditionally cooked longer, but this recipe leaves the peas al dente. If you prefer to cook them for longer, add a little more stock and cook for an additional 20 to 30 minutes.

INGREDIENTS

2 tablespoons unsalted butter

1 onion, diced

1 carrot, peeled and diced

1 celery stalk, diced

5 cups chicken stock (see page 14)

1 cup split peas

6 oz. smoked ham, cut into bite-sized pieces

2 sprigs parsley

1 bay leaf

1 teaspoon thyme, chopped

Salt and pepper, to taste

Parsley, leaves removed and chopped, for garnish

Lemon wedges, for garnish

1 In a medium saucepan, add the butter and cook over medium heat until melted. Add the onion, carrot, and celery and cook for 5 minutes, or until soft.

2 Add the stock, peas, ham, parsley, bay leaf, and thyme. Bring to a boil, then reduce heat so that the soup simmers. Cook for 45 minutes, or until peas are cooked through. Stir occasionally as the soup cooks and add more stock if it gets too thick.

3 Discard bay leaf and parsley sprigs. Season with salt and pepper and ladle into warm bowls. Garnish with chopped parsley and serve with lemon wedges.

Russian Pea and Barley Soup with Simple Country-Style Bread

YIELD: 4 SERVINGS • ACTIVE TIME: 45 MINUTES • TOTAL TIME: 21 HOURS

A typical Russian meal starts with appetizers, moves on to a rich bowl of soup, proceeds to an equally hearty main course, and finishes with a not-too-sweet dessert.

INGREDIENTS

For the Simple Country-style Bread

3 cups bread flour

1¼ teaspoons salt

¼ teaspoon instant yeast

1⅓ cups lukewarm water

Cornmeal, for dusting

For the Russian Pea and Barley Soup

½ cup yellow split peas, soaked overnight

¼ cup pearl barley, soaked overnight

6 cups ham stock (see page 19)

4 oz. thick-cut bacon, cubed

2 tablespoons unsalted butter

1 onion, chopped

1 garlic clove, minced

1½ cups parsnip, peeled and chopped

1 tablespoon oregano, leaves removed and chopped

Salt and pepper, to taste

1 To make the Simple Country-Style Bread, add all the ingredients to a large bowl and mix by hand until well-combined. Cover the bowl with plastic wrap and keep in a warm place for 18 hours, allowing the flavor to develop.

2 Remove the dough from the bowl, place on a floured surface, and knead. Sprinkle a cotton towel with cornmeal and place the dough, seam-side down, on the towel. Dust the dough with a bit more cornmeal and cover with another cotton kitchen towel. Let stand for 2 hours.

3 When the dough has rested for 1 hour and 30 minutes, place a cast-iron pot with a lid in a cold oven. Heat the oven to 450°F. Remove the pot from the oven and place the dough into it. Cover the pot and bake for 30 minutes.

4 Remove the lid and cook for another 15 minutes. Carefully remove the bread from pot and transfer to a wire rack. Let stand for 30 minutes before serving.

5 To make the soup, add the split peas, barley, and stock to a large saucepan and bring to a boil. Reduce the heat so that the mixture simmers.

6 In a sauté pan, add the bacon and cook over medium heat for 5 minutes, or until crispy. Remove the bacon from the pan and set aside. Leave the bacon fat in the pan.

7 Add the butter to the pan. When it is melted, add the onion and garlic and cook for 5 minutes. Add the parsnip and cook for another 5 minutes, or until the onion is slightly golden brown.

8 Add the bacon and the parsnip mixture to the saucepan and simmer for 20 minutes, or until the peas and barley are tender.

9 Stir in the oregano and season with salt and pepper. Serve in bowls with Simple Country-Style Bread.

African Peanut Soup

YIELD: 4 SERVINGS • ACTIVE TIME: 20 MINUTES • TOTAL TIME: 1 HOUR

This traditional African peanut soup gets a bit of a kick from the cayenne and the ginger, but the sweetness of the yam keeps it mellow.

INGREDIENTS

½ cup natural peanut butter

2 tablespoons tomato paste

6 cups chicken stock (see page 14)

1 onion, chopped

1-inch piece ginger, peeled and minced

2 sprigs thyme, leaves removed and chopped

1 bay leaf

⅛ teaspoon cayenne pepper, or to taste

1 sweet potato, peeled and chopped

6 fresh okra, sliced

Salt and pepper, to taste

Edible flowers, for garnish

1 In a medium saucepan, add the peanut butter and tomato paste. Slowly add the chicken stock, whisking constantly to keep lumps from forming.

2 Add the onion, ginger, thyme, bay leaf, and cayenne pepper.

3 Cook over medium heat and bring to a simmer. Cook for 30 minutes, stirring often.

4 Add the sweet potato and cook for 10 minutes. Add the okra and cook for an additional 5 minutes, or until the okra and sweet potato are tender.

5 Season with salt and pepper and serve in warmed bowls with edible flowers.

Rocky Mountain Chili

YIELD: 4 TO 6 SERVINGS • ACTIVE TIME: 30 MINUTES • TOTAL TIME: 1 HOUR

This is a great recipe to warm up with on a snowy winter day. Feel free to adjust the chili powder according to your spice threshold.

INGREDIENTS

1 tablespoon vegetable oil

1 onion, chopped

1 lb. ground turkey

2 garlic cloves, minced

1 tablespoon chili powder

1 Bouquet Garni
(see sidebar)

4 tomatoes, diced

1 (14 oz.) can tomato sauce

8 tablespoons tomato paste

1 (14 oz.) can kidney beans

1 (14 oz.) can white beans

1 (14 oz.) can black beans

Salt and pepper, to taste

Cheddar cheese, grated, for garnish

Sour cream, for garnish

Chives, chopped, for garnish

Cornbread, to serve (see page 116)

1 In a large saucepan, add the vegetable oil and cook over medium-high heat until warm.

2 Add the onion and ground turkey and cook for 5 minutes, or until meat has been browned.

3 Add the garlic and cook for 2 minutes, then add the chili powder, Bouquet Garni, tomatoes, tomato sauce, tomato paste, and beans. Bring to a boil, reduce heat so that the soup simmers and cook for 20 minutes, or until the meat is cooked through.

4 Season with salt and pepper and ladle into warmed bowls. Garnish with cheddar cheese, sour cream, and chopped chives. Serve with Cornbread.

BOUQUET GARNI: CUT A 2-INCH SECTION OF BUTCHER TWINE. TIE ONE SIDE OF THE ROPE AROUND A BAY LEAF, FRESH THYME SPRIG, AND FRESH PARSLEY, AND TIGHTLY KNOT IT. ATTACH THE OTHER END OF THE TWINE TO THE POT AND ADD THE HERBS TO THE SOUP.

Chicken and Corn Succotash Soup

YIELD: 4 SERVINGS • ACTIVE TIME: 20 MINUTES • TOTAL TIME: 1 HOUR

This soup is based on a classic Southern recipe. The addition of chicken makes this one sing, as it complements the sweetness of the corn nicely.

INGREDIENTS

¼ cup unsalted butter

4 slices of thick-cut bacon, cut into ¼-inch pieces

2 onions, chopped

2 garlic cloves, minced

2 chicken breasts, skin removed and chopped into ½-inch pieces

¼ cup all-purpose flour

4 cups chicken stock (see page 14)

4 ears of corn, kernels removed

1 (14 oz.) can kidney beans, rinsed and drained

1 cup heavy cream

3 tablespoons parsley, leaves removed and chopped

Salt and pepper, to taste

1 In a medium saucepan, add the butter and cook over medium heat until melted. Add the bacon, onions, and garlic and cook for 5 minutes. Add the chicken breasts and cook for 5 minutes.

2 Add the flour and cook, while stirring constantly, for 5 minutes.

3 Add the chicken stock slowly, whisking constantly to prevent lumps from forming.

4 Bring to a boil. Reduce heat so that the soup simmers. Add the corn kernels and kidney beans and simmer for 5 minutes.

5 Add the cream and return to a simmer. Add chopped parsley, season with salt and pepper, and serve in warm bowls.

Beef, Pork, and Lamb

Beef, pork, and lamb are the trinity of red meats when it comes to making rich, filling soups.

Beef is a magical protein that adds a lot of depth to the flavor profile of whatever soup it appears in. As the cuts are typically of lesser quality, they require long cooking to become tender. But these lesser quality cuts are your friend—not only are they less expensive, the requisite cook time adds a ton of flavor to the dish. This boost makes beef a popular ingredient in soups around the world—whether it be the various chilis of America, or Pho from Vietnam.

Pork has a very neutral flavor, which makes it a perfect companion for the variety of ingredients used to make quality soup. A favorite all over the world, you'll find a number of preparations from around the globe in this chapter.

Lamb is one of those proteins that people either love or hate. Some people are thrown off by the smell, which, admittedly, is pungent. But lamb is a meat rich in color and flavor, and a great vehicle for exotic spices and light broths. It also has a tendency to dry out, making it perfect for cooking long and slow.

Santa Fe Chili with Cornbread

YIELD: 4 SERVINGS • ACTIVE TIME: 45 MINUTES • TOTAL TIME: 3½ HOURS

This is the perfect dish for a get-together. The cornbread recipe is adapted from a corn muffin from the Culinary Institute of America. It's nice and moist.

INGREDIENTS

For the Santa Fe Chili
1 tablespoon vegetable oil

1 lb. beef shanks, bone-in

1 onion, peeled and chopped

1 cup corn kernels

½ cup green bell pepper, chopped

½ teaspoon ground cumin

2 garlic cloves, minced

1 tablespoon tomato paste

6 cups beef or veal stock (see page 12)

1 tomato, concasse (see sidebar)

⅛ teaspoon red pepper flakes

⅛ teaspoon Tabasco™

Salt and pepper, to taste

For the Cornbread
1 large egg

¾ cup milk

½ cup vegetable oil

½ cup sugar, plus 3 tablespoons

1 cup all-purpose flour

⅓ cup cornmeal, plus 2 tablespoons

1 teaspoon salt

1 teaspoon baking powder

For the Spiced Butter
1 cup unsalted butter, softened

1 teaspoon cinnamon

½ teaspoon ground ginger

¼ teaspoon ground cloves

¼ teaspoon nutmeg

Salt, to taste

1 In a large saucepan, add the oil and beef shanks and cook over medium heat for 5 minutes on each side, or until lightly browned.

2 Remove the beef shanks from the pan and set aside. Add the onion and cook for 3 minutes.

3 Add the corn kernels, bell pepper, cumin, and garlic and cook for 3 minutes, or until the vegetables are soft.

4 Reduce heat and return the beef shanks to the pan. Add the tomato paste and stock and allow soup to simmer for 2 hours, or until the meat is tender.

5 While the soup is simmering, start the Cornbread. Preheat oven to 375°F. In a mixer, combine the egg, milk, and oil and mix on low speed. Meanwhile, sieve your dry ingredients together.

6 Slowly incorporate the dry mixture into the egg mixture. Pour the batter into a buttered and floured 8-inch cast-iron pan. Place in oven and cook for 30 minutes, or until a cake tester or toothpick comes out clean.

7 Remove the beef shanks from the soup. Cut the meat from the bone and chop into $1/2$-inch pieces. Return meat to the soup. Add the tomato and simmer for 10 minutes.

8 While the soup is simmering, prepare the Spiced Butter by combining the butter and spices in the bowl of a standing mixer. Whip for 5 minutes, season to taste, and chill until ready to use.

9 Skim any fat off the top of the soup. Add the red pepper flakes, Tabasco™, salt, and pepper and serve in bowls with the Cornbread and Spiced Butter.

TOMATO CONCASSE: BOIL ENOUGH WATER TO SUBMERGE A TOMATO AND ADD A PINCH OF SALT. WHILE IT IS HEATING, PREPARE AN ICE BATH AND SCORE THE TOP OF THE TOMATO WITH A PARING KNIFE, TAKING CARE NOT TO CUT INTO THE MEAT OF THE TOMATO. PLACE THE TOMATO IN THE BOILING WATER FOR 30 SECONDS, OR UNTIL THE SKIN BEGINS TO BLISTER. CAREFULLY REMOVE IT FROM THE BOILING WATER AND PLACE IT IN THE ICE BATH. ONCE THE TOMATO IS COOL, REMOVE IT FROM THE ICE BATH AND USE A PARING KNIFE TO PEEL THE SKIN OFF, STARTING AT THE SCORED TOP. CUT THE TOMATO INTO QUARTERS, REMOVE THE SEEDS, AND CUT ACCORDING TO INSTRUCTIONS.

Cincinnati Chili

The chocolate works as a seasoning here, rounding out the flavor rather than taking over.

INGREDIENTS

2 tablespoons vegetable oil

1 onion, peeled and chopped

1½ lbs. ground beef

2 tablespoons chili powder, or to taste

1 teaspoon cinnamon

1 teaspoon cumin

¼ teaspoon allspice

¼ teaspoon ground cloves

2 bay leaves

2 cups beef stock (see page 12)

1 cup tomato sauce

2 tablespoons apple cider vinegar

¼ teaspoon cayenne pepper

1 oz. unsweetened chocolate

Salt and pepper, to taste

Spaghetti, cooked to taste, to serve

Cheddar cheese, grated, for garnish

Parsley, chopped, for garnish

1 In a medium saucepan, add the vegetable oil and cook over medium heat until warm. Add the onion and cook for 5 minutes, or until soft. Add the beef and use a wooden spoon to break it up as it cooks. Cook for 5 minutes, or until evenly browned.

2 Add the spices and herbs, beef stock, tomato sauce, vinegar, and cayenne pepper and bring to a boil. Reduce heat to low, cover, and cook for 1 hour, stirring occasionally.

3 Right before serving, remove from heat, add the chocolate, and season with salt and pepper.

4 Place a bed of spaghetti in a bowl. Pour chili on top, garnish with cheddar cheese, additional spaghetti, and parsley and serve.

Beef and Braised Cabbage Soup with Horseradish Cream

YIELD: 6 SERVINGS • ACTIVE TIME: 30 MINUTES • TOTAL TIME: 2½ HOURS

Consider bringing this to your next potluck dinner, as it's great with or without the steak. It also pairs well with game meats.

INGREDIENTS

For the Beef and Braised Cabbage Soup

2 lbs. red cabbage, core removed, grated

2 onions, peeled and finely sliced

1 large apple, peeled, cored, and chopped

3 tablespoons soft brown sugar

2 garlic cloves, minced

¼ teaspoon grated nutmeg

½ teaspoon caraway seeds

3 tablespoons apple cider vinegar

4 cups veal stock (see page 12)

Salt and pepper, to taste

2 tablespoons extra virgin olive oil

1½ lbs. sirloin steak, fat removed

Watercress, for garnish

For the Horseradish Cream

2 tablespoons fresh horseradish, peeled and grated

2 teaspoons white wine vinegar

½ teaspoon Dijon mustard

1 cup heavy cream

Salt and pepper, to taste

1 Preheat oven to 300°F. In a mixing bowl, add the cabbage, onions, apple, brown sugar, garlic, nutmeg, caraway seeds, and vinegar with a ½ cup of the stock. Mix until well-combined.

2 Season with salt and pepper and transfer to a large, buttered casserole dish. Cover the pan and place it in the oven. Cook for 1 hour and 30 minutes, removing to stir the contents of the casserole dish.

3 Turn off the oven and open the oven door slightly. When the dish has cooled slightly, remove it from the oven and set aside. Preheat oven to 450°F.

4 In a medium sauté pan, add the olive oil and warm over medium heat. Season the sirloin with salt and pepper and then add to pan. Cook until golden brown on both sides. Remove sirloin from the pan and set aside.

5 Spoon the cabbage dish into a large saucepan. Add the remaining stock and bring to a boil. Reduce heat so that the soup simmers.

6 Place the sirloin in the oven and cook until it is the desired level of doneness. Remove the sirloin from the oven and let it stand for 5 minutes.

7 While the sirloin is resting, make the Horseradish Cream by combining the horseradish, vinegar, mustard, and 4 tablespoons of cream in a mixing bowl. Lightly whip the remaining cream and then fold into the horseradish mixture. Season to taste.

8 Ladle the soup into serving bowls. Thinly slice the steak and place it on top of the soup. Serve with Horseradish Cream and garnish with watercress.

Mexican Beef Chili with Nachos

YIELD: 4 SERVINGS • ACTIVE TIME: 20 MINUTES
TOTAL TIME: 1 HOUR AND 15 MINUTES

Filled with beans, beef, and Mexican flavors, whip this up, open a couple of Coronas, and enjoy the game with your friends and family.

INGREDIENTS

3 tablespoons extra virgin olive oil

16 oz. beef round roast, cubed

3 onions, peeled and chopped

3 garlic cloves, minced

2 red chilies, seeded and diced

1 teaspoon cayenne pepper

1 teaspoon ground cumin

6 cups beef or veal stock (see page 12)

2 bay leaves

3 tablespoons tomato paste

1 (14 oz.) can cannellini beans, drained and rinsed

1 (14 oz.) can black beans, drained and rinsed

1 bag tortilla chips

8 oz. Monterey Jack cheese, grated

1 jalapeño, sliced

Sour cream, to taste

Cilantro, chopped, to taste

Salt and pepper, to taste

1 In a large pan, add the oil and the roast and cook over medium-high heat until the meat is golden-brown.

2 Reduce the heat. Add the onions, garlic, and chilies and cook for 5 minutes, or until soft. Add the cayenne pepper and cumin, cook for 2 minutes, and then add the beef stock, bay leaves, and tomato paste.

3 Bring to a boil, reduce heat so that the soup simmers, and cook for 30 to 40 minutes, or until the meat is tender.

4 Meanwhile, preheat oven to 350°F. Place $1/3$ of the cannellini beans and black beans in a bowl and mash them with a fork. Once the meat is tender, add the mashed beans, which will help thicken the soup.

5 On a baking tray, lay out the tortilla chips. Sprinkle with cheese and jalapeño slices, and place in the oven. Cook for 5 minutes, or until cheese is melted. Remove from oven and top with sour cream and cilantro.

6 Add the remaining beans to the soup. Adjust seasoning to taste and then serve in warmed bowls with the nachos.

Beef and Lamb Stew with Long-Grain Rice

YIELD: 4 SERVINGS • ACTIVE TIME: 30 MINUTES • TOTAL TIME: 1½ HOURS

This is a traditional Jewish chamin, a stew-like dish served at the Shabbat morning meal in Sephardi homes. This recipe combines meats and chickpeas and cooks slowly in the oven for over an hour, in order to get every ounce of flavor into the soup.

INGREDIENTS

For the Beef and Lamb Stew

½ cup chickpeas, soaked overnight

1½ tablespoons extra virgin olive oil

1 small onion, peeled and chopped

5 garlic cloves, minced

¾ cup parsnip, sliced

¾ cup carrots, peeled and sliced

1 teaspoon cumin

¼ teaspoon turmeric

1½ tablespoons fresh ginger root, peeled and minced

5 oz. brisket, cleaned and cut into ¼-inch cubes

5 oz. lamb shoulder, cleaned and cut into ¼-inch cubes

4 cups beef or veal stock (see page 12)

1 small potato, peeled and cut into chunks

1 small zucchini, sliced

8 oz. fresh tomato, diced

2 tablespoons brown lentils

1 bay leaf

½ bunch of fresh cilantro, chopped

Salt and pepper, to taste

Lemon wedges, for garnish

Fresh chilies, chopped, for garnish

For the Long-Grain Rice

2 cups water

1 teaspoon salt

1 cup long-grain rice

1 Preheat oven to 250°F. Drain the chickpeas. Place the oil in a Dutch oven and cook over medium heat until warm. Add the onion, garlic, parsnip, carrots, cumin, turmeric, and ginger and cook for 2 minutes.

2 Add the brisket and lamb and cook for 5 minutes, or until all sides are browned. Add the stock and bring to a simmer. Add the chickpeas, potato, zucchini, tomatoes, lentils, bay leaf, and cilantro. Cover, place in the oven, and cook for 1 hour and 15 minutes, or until the meat is tender.

3 Begin cooking the Long-Grain Rice 30 minutes before serving. In a medium saucepan, bring the water and salt to a boil. Add the rice, reduce heat to low, cover, and cook for 15 minutes while stirring occasionally. Turn off flame, and let stand for 5 minutes before serving.

4 Once the stew is ready, remove the lid and skim the fat from the top of the soup. Season with salt and pepper and ladle into warmed bowls with the rice. Serve with lemon wedges and garnish with the chilies.

Beef, Barley, and Portobello Mushroom Soup

YIELD: 4 TO 6 SERVINGS • ACTIVE TIME: 20 MINUTES • TOTAL TIME: 2 HOURS

This simple and easy soup is even better the next day, so be sure to make enough. This pairs best with a warmed, cheesy polenta.

INGREDIENTS

- 1 tablespoon vegetable oil
- 1¾ lb. beef stew meat, cut into 1-inch pieces
- 1 onion, chopped
- 2 celery stalks, chopped
- 2 carrots, peeled and chopped
- ½ cup red wine
- 1 garlic clove, minced
- 2 sprigs thyme, leaves removed and chopped
- 8 cups beef or veal stock (see page 12)
- ¾ cup pearl barley
- 1 lb. portobello mushrooms, sliced
- Salt and pepper, to taste

1 In a large sauce pan, warm the oil on medium-high heat. Add the beef and cook for 5 minutes, or until evenly browned. Remove with a slotted spoon and reserve.

2 Add the onion, celery, and carrots and cook for 5 minutes or until soft. Add the red wine, garlic, and thyme and reduce by half.

3 Add the seared beef, the stock, and the barley and bring to a boil. Reduce to a simmer, cover, and cook on low heat for 1 hour and 30 minutes. Add the mushrooms and cook for 10 minutes or until the beef is very tender.

4 Season with salt and pepper and serve in warmed bowls.

Tanuki Jiru

YIELD: 4 SERVINGS • ACTIVE TIME: 20 MINUTES • TOTAL TIME: 40 MINUTES

This soup was traditionally made with raccoon in Japan, but nowadays pork is the go-to protein.

INGREDIENTS

For the Daikon Salad

3-inch piece daikon

1 tablespoon sesame seeds, toasted

2 tablespoons scallion greens, chopped

1 teaspoon sesame oil

1 teaspoon soy sauce

For the Tanuki Jiru

2 tablespoons sesame oil

8 oz. boneless pork loin, sliced thin, trimmed into 1-inch pieces

6-inch piece of burdock root (if unavailable, use parsnips), peeled and sliced

½ cup daikon, chopped

4 shiitake mushrooms, stalks removed and sliced

2½ cups fish stock (see page 20)

¾ cup tofu, chopped

4 tablespoons miso

Salt and pepper, to taste

Scallions, chopped, for garnish

1 To make the Daikon Salad, place all of the ingredients in a mixing bowl and stir until combined. Place in the refrigerator for at least 10 minutes before serving.

2 To make the Tanuki Jiru, place the sesame oil in a medium saucepan and cook over medium heat until it starts to smoke.

3 Add the pork, burdock root/parsnips, daikon, and shiitake mushrooms. Cook for 5 minutes.

4 Once the pork is cooked through, add the fish stock and tofu. Bring to a boil. Reduce heat so that the soup simmers and cook for 10 minutes.

5 Place the miso in a bowl. Add 4 tablespoons of the broth and stir to make a smooth paste. Stir ⅓ of the miso mixture into the soup. Taste and add more if desired.

6 Season with salt and pepper, ladle into bowls, garnish with scallions, and serve with Daikon Salad.

Pozole

YIELD: 8 SERVINGS • ACTIVE TIME: 30 MINUTES
TOTAL TIME: 14 HOURS AND 15 MINUTES

Pozole means "hominy," which is a key ingredient in this rich stew. This traditional Mexican soup once had ritual significance, in part because it tastes divine. When you're soaking the hominy, make sure you change the water a few times.

1 Place oil in a large saucepan and cook over medium-high heat until warm. Add pork and onion and season with salt and pepper. Cook, while stirring occasionally, for 15 minutes or until pork and onion are browned.

2 Add chipotles, hominy, thyme, and cumin.

3 Add water to cover everything by about an inch. Bring to a boil and then reduce heat so that the soup simmers.

4 Cook, while stirring occasionally, until the pork and hominy are tender, at least 1¹⁄₂ hours. Add more water if necessary.

5 Stir in the garlic and cook for a few more minutes. Adjust seasoning, ladle into bowls, and garnish with cilantro and lime wedges.

INGREDIENTS

2 tablespoons vegetable oil

2 lbs. pork butt, cut into 1-inch chunks

1 large onion, chopped

Salt and pepper, to taste

4 dried chipotle peppers, halved, seeds removed, cut into ½-inch pieces

2 cups dried hominy, soaked for 12 hours

2 tablespoons thyme, leaves removed and chopped

2 tablespoons cumin

2 tablespoons garlic, minced

Cilantro, chopped, for garnish

Lime wedges, for garnish

Sweet and Sour Pork Soup

YIELD: 4 SERVINGS • ACTIVE TIME: 15 MINUTES • TOTAL TIME: 45 MINUTES

The sour comes from the tamarind and lime and the sweet comes from the honey—this is a perfect flavor profile for pork.

INGREDIENTS

2 shallots, diced

2 garlic cloves, minced

½ teaspoon black peppercorns

2 teaspoons shrimp paste

1-inch piece ginger, peeled and minced

½ cup water

1 teaspoon sugar

1 teaspoon tamarind concentrate

1 tablespoon vegetable oil

4 cups chicken stock (see page 14)

1 lb. pork tenderloin, cut into fine, 2-inch-long strips

3 cups ripe papaya, halved, seeded, peeled, and chopped

1 teaspoon honey

Juice of 1 lime

1 small Thai chili, seeded and sliced, plus more for garnish

2 scallions, white part sliced, plus more for garnish

Salt and pepper, to taste

1 In a food processor, add the shallots, garlic, peppercorns, shrimp paste, ginger, water, sugar, and tamarind concentrate. Blend into a smooth paste.

2 Place the oil in a medium saucepan and cook over medium heat until warm. Add the paste and cook for 2 minutes. Add the stock and bring to a boil.

3 Reduce the heat so that the soup simmers. Add the pork and papaya and simmer for 7 to 8 minutes, until the pork is tender.

4 Add the honey, lime juice, Thai chili, and the scallions. Season with salt and pepper, ladle into warm bowls, and garnish with Thai chili and scallions.

Italian Sausage Soup

YIELD: 4 SERVINGS • ACTIVE TIME: 20 MINUTES • TOTAL TIME: 1 HOUR

This winter favorite is very easy to prepare and makes for a beautiful, filling main course.

1 In a medium saucepan, add the olive oil and cook over medium heat until warm.

2 Add the sausage and cook for 5 minutes, or until evenly browned.

3 Use a slotted spoon to remove the sausage. Set aside.

4 Add the onion, carrots, celery, and garlic to the pan and cook for 5 minutes, or until soft.

5 Add the stock and bring to a boil. Reduce heat so that the soup simmers and cook for 10 minutes.

6 Add the zucchini, tomatoes, and beans and cook for 15 minutes.

7 Cut the cooked sausage into 1⁄4-inch slices. Add sausage and spinach to the saucepan and simmer for 5 minutes.

8 Season with salt and pepper and serve in warm bowls.

INGREDIENTS

2 tablespoons extra virgin olive oil

1 lb. hot Italian sausage

1 onion, chopped

2 carrots, chopped

1 celery stalk, chopped

2 garlic cloves, minced

6 cups beef stock (see page 12)

1 zucchini, quartered, seeds removed, and chopped

1 (14 oz.) can stewed tomatoes

1 (14 oz.) can cannellini beans

2 cups spinach

Salt and pepper, to taste

Swedish Meatball Soup

YIELD: 4 TO 6 SERVINGS • ACTIVE TIME: 30 MINUTES
TOTAL TIME: 1 HOUR AND 15 MINUTES

Swedish meatballs are a meal on their own. Cook them in a nice, seasoned broth and they become an ideal dinner option.

INGREDIENTS

For the Swedish Meatballs

1 cup panko bread crumbs

½ cup heavy cream

2 tablespoons extra virgin olive oil

1 onion, chopped

8 oz. ground beef

8 oz. ground pork

1 egg

⅛ teaspoon allspice

Salt and pepper, to taste

For the Soup

¼ cup unsalted butter

2 carrots, peeled and chopped

2 celery stalks, chopped

2 cups button mushrooms, thinly sliced

2 garlic cloves, minced

⅓ cup all-purpose flour

6 cups beef stock (see page 12)

¾ cup heavy cream

1 teaspoon Worcestershire sauce

½ teaspoon paprika

½ teaspoon red pepper flakes

Salt and pepper, to taste

Parsley, chopped, for garnish

1 To make the meatballs, add the bread crumbs and cream to a mixing bowl. Let the bread soak for 10 minutes. In a small sauté pan, add 1 tablespoon of the oil and warm over medium heat. Add the onion and cook for 5 minutes, or until soft. Turn off the heat and let the onion cool.

2 Once cool, add the cooked onion to the mixing bowl. Add the remaining ingredients and stir until well-combined. Place a small amount of the mixture in the microwave or cook a small amount on the stove. Taste and adjust seasoning accordingly.

3 Divide the mixture into 24 piles and roll each one into a nice, round ball. In a large saucepan, add the remaining oil and cook over medium-high heat until warm.

4 Add the meatballs to the pan and cook for 5 minutes, while stirring constantly. When they are golden brown all over, remove and set aside.

5 To make the soup, add the butter to a large saucepan and cook over medium heat until warm. Add the carrots and celery and cook for 3 minutes. Add the mushrooms and garlic and cook for 3 more minutes, or until the celery and carrots are soft.

6 Add the flour and cook for 3 minutes. Slowly add the beef stock to the pan, stirring constantly to prevent any lumps from forming. Bring to a boil. Reduce heat so that the soup simmers, add the Swedish Meatballs, and cook for 15 minutes, or until meatballs are cooked through.

7 Add the cream, Worcestershire sauce, paprika, and red pepper flakes. Cook for 5 minutes, season with salt and pepper, ladle into bowls, and garnish with parsley.

Lamb and Cannellini Soup

YIELD: 4 TO 6 SERVINGS • ACTIVE TIME: 20 MINUTE • TOTAL TIME: 9½ HOURS

The flavors of Greece are showcased in this lively soup.

INGREDIENTS

2 tablespoons extra virgin olive oil

1 onion, chopped

2 garlic cloves, minced

1½ lbs. ground lamb

3 carrots, peeled and chopped

3 celery stalks, chopped

1 (14 oz.) can stewed tomatoes

¼ cup parsley, leaves removed and chopped

2 sprigs thyme, leaves removed and chopped

8 oz. cannellini beans, soaked in water overnight

6 cups chicken stock (see page 14)

8 oz. baby spinach

¼ cup Kalamata olives, sliced

Salt and pepper, to taste

Feta cheese, for garnish

1 In a large saucepan, add the olive oil and cook over medium heat until warm. Add the onion and cook for 5 minutes, or until soft. Then, add the garlic and cook for an additional 2 minutes.

2 Add the lamb and cook for 3 to 4 minutes. Add the carrots and celery and cook for an additional 5 minutes.

3 Stir in the tomatoes, herbs, cannellini beans, and chicken stock. Bring to a boil, reduce heat so that the soup simmers, cover, and cook for 1 hour, or until the beans are tender.

4 Add the spinach and olives. Cook for 2 minutes, or until spinach is wilted. Season with salt and pepper and serve in warmed bowls with a sprinkle of feta cheese.

Fresh Cucumber and Lamb Broth

YIELD: 4 SERVINGS • ACTIVE TIME: 20 MINUTES • TOTAL TIME: 45 MINUTES

This very quick, light, and refreshing soup is great for a lunch or appetizer, especially on a hot day.

INGREDIENTS

1 lb. lamb loin, cut into ½-inch pieces

2 tablespoons soy sauce

2 tablespoons mirin

1 teaspoon sesame oil

4 cups chicken stock (see page 14)

1 piece lemongrass, bruised with the back of a knife

6-inch piece of cucumber, halved and cut into ⅛-inch slices

4 scallions, sliced, green pieces reserved for garnish

4 teaspoons rice wine vinegar

Salt and pepper, to taste

Cilantro, chopped, for garnish

1 lime, quartered, for garnish

1 In a small bowl, combine the lamb loin, soy sauce, mirin, and sesame oil and let marinate for 20 minutes.

2 In a medium saucepan, add the chicken stock and lemongrass and bring to a boil.

3 Reduce the heat so that the broth simmers, add the marinated lamb, and cook for 2 minutes.

4 Add the cucumber slices and scallion whites and cook for an additional 2 minutes.

5 Season with the rice wine vinegar, salt, and pepper and serve in warmed bowls with the scallion greens, cilantro, and lime.

Lamb Shank and Barley Soup with Fondant Potatoes

YIELD: 4 TO 6 SERVINGS • ACTIVE TIME: 30 MINUTES • TOTAL TIME: 2 HOURS

This warming soup is packed with slow-cooked lamb, fresh vegetables, and barley, making it more like a stew than a soup.

INGREDIENTS

For the Lamb Shank and Barley Soup

2 tablespoons vegetable oil

2 lamb shanks, trimmed

1 onion, peeled and chopped

2 garlic cloves, crushed

2 carrots, peeled and chopped

2 celery stalks, chopped

1 leek, white part only, sliced

½ cup red wine

8 cups lamb or beef stock (see page 12)

½ cup pearl barley

1½ tablespoons rosemary, chopped

For the Fondant Potato

¼ cup unsalted butter

2 potatoes, sliced into 1-inch thick pieces and cut with a ring cutter

Salt and pepper, to taste

1 To make the soup, add the oil to a large saucepan and cook over medium heat until warm. Add the lamb shanks and cook until they are browned evenly. Remove the lamb shanks and set aside.

2 Add the onion, garlic, carrots, celery, and leek and cook for 5 minutes, or until soft. Add the red wine and cook for an additional 5 minutes.

3 Return the lamb shanks to the pan. Add the stock, pearl barley, and 1 tablespoon of the rosemary. Bring to a boil, reduce the heat so that the soup simmers, cover, and cook for 1 hour and 30 minutes, or until the meat is very tender and falling off the bone.

4 Remove the shanks and allow to cool slightly. Remove the meat off the bone and cut into pieces. Return the meat to the soup, add the remaining rosemary, season to taste, and ladle into bowls.

5 To make the Fondant Potatoes, in a small saucepan, add the butter and cook over low heat until melted. Add the potatoes and cook for 10 minutes on one side, or until golden brown.

6 Turn the potatoes over and cook for another 5 minutes, or until it's golden brown and the butter starts browning and gives off a nutty fragrance. Remove, season with salt and pepper, place in the bowls of soup, and serve.

Bread Soup with Pita Bread

YIELD: 6 SERVINGS • ACTIVE TIME: 30 MINUTES • TOTAL TIME: 3½ HOURS

Traditionally, this Egyptian soup, employed on a feast day 72 days after Ramadan, is made from the meat and bones of a sacrificial lamb.

INGREDIENTS

For the Pita Bread

1½ cups bread flour

1 teaspoon instant yeast

½ teaspoon sugar

¾ teaspoon salt

¾ cup water

1 tablespoon vegetable oil

For the Bread Soup

2 marrow bones

1 lb. lamb shoulder, cleaned and cubed

⅓ cup long-grain rice, rinsed

3 garlic cloves, minced

3 tablespoons unsalted butter

3 tablespoons white wine vinegar

3 tablespoons parsley, chopped, for garnish

1 To make the Pita Bread, preheat oven to 500°F. Combine all the ingredients in a mixing bowl and mix to form a dough. Place the dough on a lightly floured surface and knead until smooth. Place the dough in a lightly greased bowl and cover it with a towel. Let it stand until it nearly doubles in size and is quite puffy.

2 Place the dough on a lightly oiled work surface and divide into 4 pieces. Roll the pieces into 6-inch circles and place them on a lightly greased baking tray. Allow them to stand for 15 minutes.

3 Place the baking tray on the lowest rack in your oven and bake for 5 minutes, or until the bread has puffed up. Move the tray to a higher rack and bake for an additional 5 minutes, or until the bread is golden brown on top. Remove from the oven and set aside.

4 To make the Bread Soup, add the bones and enough water to cover them by one inch in a large stockpot. Bring to a boil and cook the marrow bones for 5 minutes. Remove the bones, submerge them in cold water, and discard the cooking water.

5 Return the blanched bones to the stockpot and cover with the same amount of fresh water. Bring to a boil, then reduce the heat so that the water simmers.

6 Add the lamb shoulder and cook for 2 hours, or until the meat is tender. Add water if necessary, as the bones and meat should always be submerged. Remove the marrow bones 20 minutes before serving and add the rice. Simmer for 10 minutes, or until the rice is cooked.

7 In a small saucepan, cook the garlic and butter over low heat until fragrant. Add the white wine vinegar and bring to a boil.

8 Split open the pita bread and toast under a broiler, turning once, until both sides are crispy and lightly browned. Place the pita on the bottom of warmed soup bowls.

9 Pour the garlic-and-vinegar mixture over the pita bread. Adjust the seasoning of the soup, pour it into the serving bowls, and garnish with parsley.

Poultry

Chicken seems to be made for soup, to the point that chicken soup is synonymous with comfort, and is still our best answer for the common cold. However, there are a number of other fowl that are wonderful in soups, such as guinea hen, quail, and turkey. This chapter includes recipes that feature the lean, flavorful meat from some of the more common winged creatures that make their way to the dinner table.

Chicken Noodle Soup

A soup cookbook would be incomplete without this classic. It's simple, quick, and you probably already have all the ingredients in your house.

INGREDIENTS

1 tablespoon vegetable oil

½ onion, diced

1 carrot, peeled and diced

1 celery stalk, diced

1 sprig thyme, leaves removed and chopped

4 cups chicken stock (see page 14)

Salt and pepper, to taste

1½ cups medium egg noodles

1 chicken breast, seared and cooked through

1 Place the oil in a medium saucepan and cook over medium heat until warm. Add the onion and cook for 5 minutes, or until soft. Add the remaining vegetables and cook until tender.

2 Add the thyme and chicken stock and bring to a boil. Reduce heat so that the soup simmers and cook for 20 minutes. Season with salt and pepper.

3 Bring to a boil, add the egg noodles, and cook for 7 minutes, or until the noodles reach the desired tenderness.

4 Chop the seared chicken breast into $1/2$-inch pieces and add to the soup. Serve in warm bowls.

Lemon Turkey Couscous Soup

YIELD: 4 SERVINGS • ACTIVE TIME: 20 MINUTES • TOTAL TIME: 1 HOUR

Feeling a bit lethargic after your Thanksgiving meal? Whip up this light, leftover turkey soup for lunch the next day. To make the turkey stock, follow the steps of chicken stock but substitute turkey.

1 In a medium saucepan, add the olive oil and cook over medium heat until warm. Add the onion and cook for 5 minutes, or until soft.

2 Add the garlic and cook for 2 minutes. Add the carrots, celery, and bell peppers and cook for 5 minutes, or until tender. Add the stock, lemon zest, and couscous and bring to a boil.

3 Reduce heat so that the soup simmers and cook for 15 minutes.

4 Add the cooked turkey and lemon juice and simmer for 5 minutes.

5 Add the spinach and cook for 2 minutes, or until wilted. Season with salt and pepper and serve in warm bowls.

INGREDIENTS

2 tablespoons extra virgin olive oil

1 onion, chopped

2 garlic cloves

2 carrots, peeled and diced

2 celery stalks, diced

⅓ cup red bell pepper, diced

⅓ cup green bell pepper, diced

6 cups turkey stock (see page 14)

Zest and juice of 1 lemon

½ cup Israeli couscous

2 cups cooked turkey meat, chopped

4 cups spinach

Salt and pepper, to taste

Southwestern Chicken Soup

YIELD: 4 SERVINGS • ACTIVE TIME: 15 MINUTES • TOTAL TIME: 45 MINUTES

Rich and creamy avocados are the key to this soup. Serve it with cornbread and you'll be hard pressed to find any leftovers.

INGREDIENTS

2 cups cooked chicken meat, diced

4 cups chicken stock (see page 14)

2 (14 oz.) cans stewed tomatoes

½ jalapeño, seeds removed and chopped

2 plum tomatoes, chopped

1 onion, chopped

2 garlic cloves, minced

Juice of 1 lime

½ teaspoon cayenne pepper

½ teaspoon ground cumin

2 ripe avocados, peeled and chopped

Salt and pepper, to taste

Sour cream, for garnish

Cilantro, chopped, for garnish

1 cup Monterey Jack cheese, grated, for garnish

Cornbread, to serve (see page 116)

1 In a large saucepan, add the chicken, stock, stewed tomatoes, jalapeño, plum tomatoes, onion, garlic, lime juice, cayenne pepper, and cumin and bring to a boil.

2 Reduce heat so that the soup simmers and cook for 25 minutes.

3 Stir in the avocado and simmer for 10 minutes, or until the soup thickens slightly.

4 Season with salt and pepper, ladle into warm bowls, garnish with sour cream, cilantro, and Monterey Jack cheese, and serve with cornbread.

Mulligatawny Chicken Curry Soup with Curried Cashews

YIELD: 4 SERVINGS • ACTIVE TIME: 20 MINUTES • TOTAL TIME: 1 HOUR

When Anglicized, the Tamil words for "pepper water" become the name of this soup. It was so popular with the English living in India during the colonial era that it was one of the few Indian dishes mentioned in the literature of the period.

INGREDIENTS

For the Curried Cashews

2 tablespoons unsalted butter

½ cup unsalted raw cashews

1 teaspoon curry powder

Salt, to taste

For the Mulligatawny Chicken Curry Soup

1 onion, chopped

2 carrots, peeled and chopped

2 celery stalks, chopped

¼ cup unsalted butter

2 tablespoons all-purpose flour

1 tablespoon curry powder

1 tablespoon poppy seeds

1 teaspoon cumin

4 cups chicken stock (see page 14)

⅓ cup long-grain rice

1 apple, peeled, cored, and chopped

1 cup cooked chicken leg meat, chopped

¼ teaspoon dried thyme

½ cup heavy cream

Salt and pepper, to taste

Cilantro, for garnish

1 To make the Curried Cashews, add the butter to a small sauté pan and cook over medium heat until melted. Add the cashews and cook for 4 minutes, while stirring constantly.

2 Add the curry powder and cook until the cashews are golden brown. Remove, set on a paper towel, season with salt, and reserve until ready to serve.

3 In a large stockpot, add the onion, carrots, celery, and butter and cook over medium heat for 5 minutes, or until soft. Stir in the flour, curry, poppy seeds, and cumin and cook for 3 minutes. Pour in the chicken stock and bring to a boil.

4 Add the rice, reduce heat so that the soup simmers, and cook for 15 minutes. Add in the apple, chicken, and thyme and simmer for 10 more minutes.

5 Add the cream, return to a simmer, season with salt and pepper, garnish with cilantro, and serve with Curried Cashews.

Guinea Hen and Roasted Grape Stew

YIELD: 4 SERVINGS • ACTIVE TIME: 20 MINUTES • TOTAL TIME: 1½ HOURS

In this stew, the meat becomes very tender, paring perfectly with the mushrooms and roasted grapes.

INGREDIENTS

For the Guinea Hen and Roasted Grape Stew

⅓ cup all-purpose flour

2 guinea hens, breasts and legs removed

6 strips thick-cut bacon, cut into 1-inch cubes

2 cups red grapes

1 cup white wine

1 cup Riesling

1 cup wild mushrooms, sliced

1 onion, chopped

2 carrots, peeled and chopped

1 cup orange juice

2 cups chicken stock (see page 14)

Salt and pepper, to taste

For the Long-Grain Rice

2 cups water

1 teaspoon salt

1 cup long-grain rice

1 Preheat oven to 350°F. In a mixing bowl, add the flour and pieces of guinea hen. Gently toss until the meat is coated.

2 Warm a cast-iron pan over medium heat. Add the bacon, cook until bacon is crispy, remove with a slotted spoon, and set aside. Add the pieces of guinea hen and cook for 5 minutes, or until evenly browned.

3 Remove with a slotted spoon and set aside with the bacon. Add the grapes, white wine, and Riesling and cook for 5 minutes, or until reduced by half.

4 Remove the grapes and set aside with the bacon and guinea hen. Add the remaining ingredients, bring to a simmer, and then place in the oven. Bake for 20 minutes.

5 While the hen bakes, prepare the Long-Grain Rice. In a medium saucepan, bring the water and salt to a boil. Add the rice, reduce heat to low, cover, and cook for 15 minutes while stirring occasionally. Turn off the flame, and let stand for 5 minutes before serving.

6 Return the bacon, guinea hen, and grapes to the pan and continue to cook for 30 minutes, or until the guinea hen is cooked and the vegetables are tender. Season with salt and pepper and serve with the Long-Grain Rice.

Velvety Chicken and Chestnut Soup

YIELD: 4 SERVINGS • ACTIVE TIME: 45 MINUTES
TOTAL TIME: 28 HOURS AND 45 MINUTES

The time required is mainly spent on the stock and drying out the chestnuts, so if you prepare those in advance it's a fast soup.

INGREDIENTS

For the Velvety Chicken and Chestnut Soup

1 lb. chestnuts

1 whole chicken (about 3½ lbs.)

2 tablespoons unsalted butter

1 carrot, peeled and diced

1 onion, diced

2 celery stalks, diced

3 rosemary sprigs, leaves removed and chopped

3 thyme sprigs, leaves removed and chopped

2 garlic cloves, chopped

1 cup Riesling

1 cup heavy cream

Salt and pepper, to taste

For the Chicken Breasts

1 teaspoon extra virgin olive oil

2 chicken breasts

Salt and pepper, to taste

2 tablespoons unsalted butter, sliced into 4 pieces

1 Score the top of each chestnut, place on a baking tray, and leave out for 1 day to dry. Preheat oven to 400°F. Cook chestnuts for 45 minutes or until nice and fragrant. Remove from oven and let cool. When cool, peel chestnuts and set aside.

2 Preheat the oven to 400°F. Remove the breasts of the chicken and set aside. Place the legs and the carcass on a baking tray and bake for 45 minutes, or until golden brown. Remove and set aside.

3 While the carcass and legs are baking, start the Chicken Breasts. Warm the oil in a heavy bottom grill pan or sauté pan on medium high heat. Once hot, gently place the chicken breasts skin side down in the pan and lower the heat to medium. Cook for 5 minutes or until the skin is nice and crispy. Flip the breast and cook for an additional 5 minutes, then season to taste.

4 Place the seared breasts on a baking tray and place two pieces of the sliced butter on top of each breast. Place in the oven and cook for 5 to 10 minutes or until cooked to desired temperature. Rest on a cutting board for 5 minutes and thinly slice.

5 Meanwhile, add the butter for the soup to a stockpot and cook over medium heat until melted. Add the carrot, onion, celery stalks, herbs, and garlic and cook for 5 minutes, or until soft. Add the Riesling and cook for 5 minutes.

6 Add the roasted legs and carcass to the saucepan, cover with water, and simmer for 2 hours, or until the stock is nice and flavorful. Strain the chicken stock through a fine sieve.

7 Place 4 cups of stock and three quarters of the peeled chestnuts in a food processor and puree until velvety. Add more chicken stock, if necessary. Chop the remaining chestnuts and reserve.

8 Place the soup in a pan, bring to a boil, and add the heavy cream. Season with salt and pepper and ladle into bowls. Garnish with the reserved chestnuts and serve with Chicken Breasts.

Coconut and Chicken Curry Soup with Naan

YIELD: 4 SERVINGS • ACTIVE TIME: 45 MINUTES • TOTAL TIME: 3½ HOURS

Here we take a traditional Indian curry and turn it into a soup. If you're worried about the level of spice, or you want more, adjust the amount of jalapeño.

INGREDIENTS

For the Naan

½ teaspoon yeast

1 cup warm water

2 teaspoons sugar

1 tablespoon milk

1 egg

1 teaspoon salt

2 cups bread flour

½ cup unsalted butter, melted

For the Coconut and Chicken Curry Soup

2 tablespoons vegetable oil

2 chicken breasts, skin-on

1 onion, chopped

1 carrot, peeled and chopped

1 garlic clove, minced

2 cups chicken stock (see page 14)

1 (14 oz.) can coconut milk

½ cup cilantro, stems and leaves chopped, plus more for garnish

2 lime leaves

1 tablespoon curry powder

½ jalapeño, seeds removed, chopped

Juice of ½ lime

Salt and pepper, to taste

Scallion greens, for garnish

Bamboo shoots, chopped, for garnish

For the Long-Grain Rice

2 cups water

1 teaspoon salt

1 cup long-grain rice

1 Begin by preparing the Naan. Combine the yeast and warm water in a bowl and let stand for 10 minutes before serving. In a separate bowl, combine the yeast mixture, sugar, milk, egg, salt, and bread flour and mix by hand until formed into a ball of dough.

2 On a lightly floured surface, knead the dough for 5 minutes. Place the dough in a bowl, cover it with a towel, and let stand for 30 to 45 minutes in a warm place, until it doubles in size. Cut into 4 pieces and roll on a lightly floured surface. Each piece should be a $1/4$-inch high.

3 Brush both sides with melted butter and cook until golden brown. Remove from the oven and set aside. Be sure to butter the Naan before serving.

4 To start the soup, add the oil to a medium saucepan and cook over medium heat until it is nice and hot. Add the chicken breasts, skin side down, and cook for 5 minutes, or until golden brown.

5 Flip the breasts and cook for an additional 5 minutes. Remove and set aside. Add the onion, carrot, and garlic to the pan and cook for 5 minutes, or until soft. Add the chicken stock and coconut milk and bring to a boil.

6 Add the cilantro, lime leaves, curry powder, and jalapeño. Reduce heat so that the soup simmers and cook for 15 minutes. Meanwhile, remove the skin from the chicken breasts and discard. Cut the breasts into 1-inch cubes. The inside should still be raw.

7 After the soup has cooked for 15 minutes, remove the lime leaves and transfer the soup to a food processor. Puree until smooth, return to the pan, and bring to a simmer. Add the chicken and lime juice, and simmer for 10 minutes, or until the chicken is cooked through.

8 While the soup simmers, prepare the Long-Grain Rice. In a medium saucepan, bring the water and salt to a boil. Add the rice, reduce heat to low, cover, and cook for 15 minutes while stirring occasionally. Turn off flame, and let stand for 5 minutes before serving.

9 Season with salt and pepper and ladle into warm bowls. Garnish with cilantro, scallion greens, and bamboo shoots, and serve with Long-Grain Rice and Naan.

Lemongrass-Scented Chicken and Rice Soup

YIELD: 4 SERVINGS • ACTIVE TIME: 30 MINUTES • TOTAL TIME: 3 HOURS

Also known as Chnor Chrook, this light and refreshing Cambodian soup awakens the senses with the chili and the citrus aroma. It is a bit spicy, so adjust to your personal taste.

INGREDIENTS

For the Naan

½ teaspoon yeast

1 cup warm water

2 teaspoons sugar

1 tablespoon milk

1 egg

1 teaspoon salt

2 cups bread flour

½ cup unsalted butter, melted

For the Lemongrass-Scented Chicken and Rice Soup

2 chicken thighs

8 cups chicken stock (see page 14)

1-inch piece of ginger, sliced

3 lemon grass stalks, cut in half and bruised with the back side of a knife

1 Thai chili with seeds

3 tablespoons fish sauce

½ cup long-grain rice, rinsed

Chili, cut into thin strips, for garnish

Chopped cilantro, for garnish

Lime wedges, for garnish

1 Begin by preparing the Naan. Combine the yeast and warm water in a bowl and let stand for 10 minutes before serving.

2 In a separate bowl, combine the yeast mixture, sugar, milk, egg, salt, and bread flour and mix by hand until it is formed into a ball of dough.

3 On a lightly floured surface, knead the dough for 5 minutes. Place the dough in a bowl, cover it with a towel, and let stand for 30 to 45 minutes in a warm place, until it doubles in size. Cut into 4 pieces and roll on a lightly floured surface. Each piece should be a ¼-inch high.

4 Brush both sides with melted butter and cook until golden brown. Remove from the oven and set aside. Be sure to butter the Naan before serving.

5 To prepare the soup, add the chicken thighs, chicken stock, ginger, lemongrass, Thai chili, and fish sauce to a large saucepan. Bring to a boil and simmer for 2 hours or until the chicken legs are tender. Skim off any fat.

6 Remove the chicken legs and pick apart the meat. Discard the skin and bones. Strain the stock through a fine sieve. Reboil stock, stir in the rice, and simmer for 30 minutes, or until rice is cooked.

7 Remove the chili, add chicken leg meat, and cook until hot. Garnish with thinly sliced chili, chopped cilantro, and lime wedges and serve with Naan.

Sweet and Hot Pepper Chicken Stew with Katsamaki

YIELD: 4 SERVINGS • ACTIVE TIME: 30 MINUTES • TOTAL TIME: 2 HOURS

This recipe was originally a Greek staple that has been incorporated into a stew. Mixing in the Katsamaki gives a great texture and mouthfeel from the cheese. It is very similar to polenta and the cheese can be replaced with any hard sheep cheese.

INGREDIENTS

For the Sweet and Hot Pepper Chicken Stew

3 tablespoons unsalted butter

1 chicken breast, skin removed, cut into ½-inch pieces

1 large onion, chopped

1 garlic clove, minced

2 green bell peppers, seeds removed and chopped

¼ teaspoon ground allspice

½ teaspoon ground cloves

½ teaspoon ground cinnamon

¼ teaspoon thyme, leaves removed and chopped

½ Thai chili, seeds removed, and diced

¼ cup Kalamata olives, sliced

4 cups chicken stock (see page 14)

1½ cups tomatoes, concasse (see page 117) and chopped

Salt and pepper, to taste

Thyme leaves, for garnish

Feta cheese, for garnish

For the Katsamaki

1¼ cups of vegetable stock (see page 25)

½ cup corn meal

1 cup grated kefalotyri cheese or hard cheese of choice

Salt and pepper, to taste

1 Heat 1 tablespoon of the butter in a large heavy bottom pan over medium heat and sear the chicken pieces for 8 minutes or until lightly browned on all sides. Remove chicken pieces with a slotted spoon and set aside.

2 Add another tablespoon of butter to the pan and cook the onions, garlic, and bell peppers for 8 minutes or until soft. Place the chicken back in the pot and add the allspice, cloves, cinnamon, thyme, and Thai chili. Stir for 2 minutes.

3 While the chicken simmers, prepare the Katsamaki. In a medium, heavy bottom pan, boil the stock. On a low flame, slowly add the corn meal, whisk nicely and cook for 4 to 5 minutes or until corn meal is cooked. Remove from heat, add the cheese. Season with salt and pepper and set aside.

4 Add the olives and chicken stock to the soup, reduce the flame to low, and simmer for 40 minutes or until the chicken is tender.

5 Add the tomatoes to the soup, and season with salt and pepper, and swirl in the remaining butter.

6 Make a circle with the Katsamaki creating a bowl for the soup. Pour the soup in the middle, garnish with thymo leaves, and sprinkle with feta cheese.

Seafood

The fun thing about this chapter is that the recipes take you on an international journey. While it is easy to get fresh seafood from far-flung bodies of water into your home, that doesn't mean you need to look beyond what is local, as most of the proteins in these recipes are easily interchangeable with what is available in your neighborhood. So please, use the recipes here as guidelines rather than hard and fast rules. You, and your cooking, will benefit from such an approach.

Creamy Haddock Chowder

YIELD: 4 SERVINGS • ACTIVE TIME: 30 MINUTES • TOTAL TIME: 2½ HOURS

This thick, satisfying soup is packed with fish and potatoes, making it perfect for the winter.

INGREDIENTS

For the Chowder Crackers

1 cup all-purpose flour

1 teaspoon salt

1 teaspoon sugar

1 teaspoon baking powder

2 tablespoons unsalted butter, cut into ¼-inch cubes

¼ cup cold water, plus 3 tablespoons

For the Creamy Haddock Chowder

4 pieces thick-cut bacon, cut into small pieces

1 large onion, chopped

4 cups potatoes, cut into ¼-inch cubes

4 cups fish stock (see page 20)

1½ lbs. haddock, skin removed, cut into ½-inch cubes

2 tablespoons parsley, leaves removed and chopped

1 tablespoon chives, chopped, plus more for garnish

1 tablespoon tarragon, leaves removed and chopped

2 cups heavy cream

Salt and pepper, to taste

1 To make the Chowder Crackers, preheat oven to 375°F. Add the flour, salt, sugar, and baking powder to a mixing bowl and whisk until combined. Add butter and mix with your hands until the mixture resembles a coarse meal. Add the water and mix until it forms a dough. Be careful not to overmix.

2 Place the dough in a lightly floured bowl and chill in the refrigerator for 15 to 20 minutes.

3 Remove the dough from the refrigerator and place on a well-floured surface. Roll out to a ¼-inch thickness, cut dough into ½-inch diamonds, and transfer to a parchment-lined baking tray.

4 Place the tray in the oven and bake for 20 minutes, or until there is just a little color around the edges. Remove and let cool on a wire rack.

5 To make the chowder, add the bacon to a medium saucepan and cook over low heat until crispy. Add the onion and potatoes and cook for 10 minutes. Add fish stock and bring to a boil.

6 Reduce the heat so that the soup simmers and cook for 10 minutes, or until the potatoes are soft. Add the haddock and the herbs and simmer for 10 minutes.

7 Add the cream and slowly return to a simmer. Season with salt and pepper, ladle into warm bowls, garnish with chives, and serve with Chowder Crackers.

Seafarers' Stew

YIELD: 4 SERVINGS • ACTIVE TIME: 30 MINUTES • TOTAL TIME: 2 HOURS

Feel free to be creative with the seafood you use in this stew. However, make sure to use a smoked fish, as its flavor is crucial to the dish.

INGREDIENTS

For the Seafarers' Stew

8 oz. smoked mackerel, skin removed, cut into ¼-inch pieces

8 oz. swordfish, cut into 1-inch cubes

4 oz. small shrimp, skins removed and deveined

3 cups lobster stock (see page 23)

3 cups fish stock (see page 20)

8 clams, cleaned

8 mussels, cleaned

1 tablespoon extra virgin olive oil

2 shallots, minced

4 pieces thick-cut bacon, cut into 1-inch pieces

3 cups carrots, peeled and grated

¾ cup heavy cream

Salt and pepper, to taste

Parsley, chopped, for garnish

For the Crispy Calamari

1 cup vegetable oil

6 calamari tentacles

2 calamari bodies, sliced into ¼-inch rings

1 cup buttermilk

½ cup all-purpose flour

½ cup cornmeal

1 teaspoon Old Bay seasoning

Salt and pepper, to taste

1 In a large saucepan over medium heat, add the mackerel, swordfish, shrimp, lobster stock, and fish stock. Bring to a simmer and cook for 5 minutes. Add the clams, cover the pan, and cook for 3 minutes. Add the mussels and cook for an additional 3 minutes, or until the mussels and clams have opened. Remove any that don't open.

2 Strain the soup through a fine sieve and reserve the broth and the solids.

3 In a large saucepan, add the oil and cook over medium-high heat until warm. Add the shallots and bacon and cook until the bacon is browned.

4 Add the broth and bring to a boil. Reduce heat so that the soup simmers, add the carrots, and cook for 5 minutes. Add the cream and the reserved solids and season to taste. Continue to simmer.

5 While the soup simmers, prepare the Crispy Calamari. Add the oil to a Dutch oven and cook over medium-high heat until oil reaches 375°F.

6 Place the calamari and the buttermilk in a bowl. Marinate for 15 minutes. Combine the flour, cornmeal, and Old Bay seasoning in a bowl. Dredge the calamari in the mixture until evenly coated.

7 Using tongs, gently place the calamari into the oil. Cook until golden brown, remove with a slotted spoon, and set on a paper towel to drain. Season with salt and pepper.

8 Ladle the stew into warmed bowls and garnish with Crispy Calamari and parsley.

New England Clam Chowder

YIELD: 4 TO 6 SERVINGS • ACTIVE TIME: 45 MINUTES • TOTAL TIME: 2 HOURS

Chopped clams, potatoes, and cream combine to make this famously rich stew.

INGREDIENTS

For the Oyster Crackers

1 cup all-purpose flour

1 teaspoon salt

1 teaspoon sugar

1 teaspoon baking powder

2 tablespoons unsalted butter, cut into ¼-inch cubes

¼ cup cold water, plus 3 tablespoons

For the New England Clam Chowder

4 lbs. steamer clams

2 cups white wine

2 cups onions, chopped

4 tablespoons unsalted butter

1 teaspoon thyme, leaves removed and chopped

2 cups Yukon Gold potatoes, peeled and chopped

4 cups heavy cream

Salt and pepper, to taste

Parsley, chopped, for garnish

1 To make the Oyster Crackers, preheat oven to 375°F.

2 Add the flour, salt, sugar, and baking powder to a mixing bowl and whisk until combined. Add the butter and mix with your hands until the mixture resembles a coarse meal. Add the water and mix until it a dough forms. Be careful not to overmix.

3 Place the dough in a lightly floured bowl and chill in the refrigerator for 15 to 20 minutes.

4 Remove the bowl from the refrigerator and place on a well-floured surface. Roll to a ¼-inch thickness, cut into small circles with a ring cutter, and transfer to a parchment-lined baking tray.

5 Bake for 20 minutes, or until there is a little color around the bottom edges of the crackers. Remove and let cool on a wire rack.

6 To make the chowder, add the clams, wine, and half of the chopped onions. Cover and cook over medium-high heat for 5 minutes, or until all the clams have opened. Strain through a fine sieve. Set the clams aside and reserve the cooking liquid.

7 In a clean medium saucepan, add the butter and cook over medium heat until melted. Add the remaining onions and cook for 5 minutes, or until soft. Add the reserved cooking liquid and thyme and bring to a simmer. Cook for 5 minutes, or until the liquid has been reduced by half.

8 Meanwhile, remove the meat from the clams. Separate the bellies and reserve. Peel the outer membrane from the clam and discard. Roughly chop the clam.

9 Add the potatoes and heavy cream to the saucepan and cook for 5 minutes, or until the potatoes are tender. Add the chopped clams and clam bellies. Season with salt and pepper, and ladle into warm bowls. Garnish with parsley and serve with Oyster Crackers.

Corn and Seafood Chowder with Salt Cod Beignets

YIELD: 4 TO 6 SERVINGS • ACTIVE TIME: 1 HOUR • TOTAL TIME: 3½ HOURS

For something utilizing the famously light fruits of the sea, this is a very rich dish.

INGREDIENTS

For the Salt Cod Beignets

½ cup milk

3 tablespoons unsalted butter

¼ cup all-purpose flour

1 egg

4 oz. salt cod, chopped

1 tablespoon cilantro, chopped

2 cups vegetable oil

Salt and pepper, to taste

For the Corn and Seafood Chowder

1½ cups corn kernels

2 cups milk

2 tablespoons unsalted butter

1 garlic clove, minced

4 strips thick-cut bacon, chopped

1 green bell pepper, seeded and chopped

¾ cups celery, chopped

½ cup long-grain rice

1 tablespoon all-purpose flour

2 cups crab stock (see page 17)

4 scallops, cut into ¼-inch thick slices

4 oz. haddock, cut into ½-inch pieces

3 oz. lobster, cut into ¼-inch pieces

2 tablespoons parsley, chopped, plus more for garnish

⅛ teaspoon cayenne pepper

1½ cups tomatoes, concasse (see page 117) and chopped

Salt and pepper, to taste

1 Begin by preparing the Salt Cod Beignets. In a small saucepan, add the milk and butter and bring to a boil. Add the flour, and stir until it forms a ball of dough. Remove the saucepan from heat and let stand for 10 minutes.

2 Add the egg slowly and whisk until well-combined. Add the salt cod and cilantro, roll into a log, wrap with plastic wrap, and place in the freezer for 2 hours.

3 Place the oil in a Dutch oven and cook over medium-high heat until 375°F. Remove the log from the freezer and cut into 1½-inch thick slices. Gently place each slice in the oil and fry until golden brown.

4 Use a slotted spoon to remove from oil and set on a paper towel to drain. Season to taste with salt and pepper, and set aside.

5 To make the chowder, in a blender, add the corn kernels and milk and puree until creamy. In a medium saucepan, add the butter and cook over medium heat until melted. Add the garlic and bacon and cook for 5 minutes. Add the green pepper and celery and sweat for 4 minutes, or until soft.

6 Add the rice and cook for 4 minutes. Add the flour and cook for 2 minutes, while stirring constantly. Gradually add the pureed corn and stock to the saucepan. Bring to a simmer and cook for 20 minutes, or until the rice is tender.

7 Stir in the scallops, haddock, and lobster. Cook for 4 minutes and then add the parsley, cayenne pepper, and tomatoes. Cook for a few more minutes, adjust the seasoning, and ladle into warm bowls. Serve with Salt Cod Beignets and garnish with parsley.

Seafood Minestrone with Basil Pesto

YIELD: 4 TO 6 SERVINGS • ACTIVE TIME: 45 MINUTES • TOTAL TIME: 1½ HOURS

This version of the classic Italian soup uses mussels, shrimp, and oysters to take it up a notch.

INGREDIENTS

For the Basil Pesto

2 cups water

1 oz. basil

2 oz. spinach

1 garlic clove, minced

2 tablespoons pine nuts

¼ cup Parmesan cheese, grated

6 tablespoons extra virgin olive oil

Salt and pepper, to taste

For the Seafood Minestrone

½ cup white wine

30 mussels, rinsed and scrubbed

1 tablespoon extra virgin olive oil

4 strips thick-cut bacon, chopped

1 garlic clove, minced

1 onion, chopped

2 celery stalks, chopped

1 tablespoon tomato paste

1 teaspoon rosemary, leaves removed and chopped

1 teaspoon thyme, leaves removed and chopped

1 bay leaf

1 teaspoon lemon juice

6 tablespoons dried kidney beans, soaked in cold water overnight

6 tablespoons Arborio rice

⅔ cup tomato, concasse (see page 117) and chopped

6 cups fish stock (see page 20)

6 oz. shrimp, peeled and deveined

12 oysters, removed from shell, juices reserved

Salt and pepper, to taste

Basil leaves, for garnish

Parmesan cheese, grated, for garnish

1 Begin by making the Basil Pesto. Bring the water to boil in a medium saucepan. Add the basil and spinach and cook for 1 minute. Remove and submerge in ice water. Drain any excess water and set aside.

2 Place basil, spinach, garlic, pine nuts, Parmesan, and olive oil into a food processor and puree until the mixture is the desired consistency. Season with salt and pepper. Refrigerate until ready to serve.

3 To make the soup, add the wine and the mussels to a large saucepan, cover, and cook over medium heat until the mussels open. Discard any that do not. Strain through a cheesecloth. Set the mussels aside and reserve the cooking liquid. Remove the mussels from their shells. Reserve a few shells for garnish.

4 In a medium saucepan, add the oil and warm over medium heat. Add the bacon and cook for 4 minutes. Add the garlic, onion, and celery and cook for 5 minutes, or until the vegetables are tender.

5 Add the tomato paste, rosemary, thyme, bay leaf, lemon juice, kidney beans, rice, and tomato and cook for 2 minutes.

6 Add the fish stock and bring to a boil. Reduce heat so that the soup simmers and cook for 12 minutes, or until the beans and rice are tender. Add the mussels, shrimp, and oysters. Season to taste and simmer for 4 minutes, or until the shrimp and oysters are cooked.

7 Ladle into warm bowls and garnish with reserved mussel shells, Basil Pesto, basil leaves, and Parmesan.

Seafood Wonton Soup

YIELD: 4 SERVINGS • ACTIVE TIME: 40 MINUTES • TOTAL TIME: 1 HOUR

Wonton soup is probably one of the most popular Chinese soups. Just the thought of this recipe is sure to make your mouth water.

INGREDIENTS

For the Seafood Wontons

4 oz. raw shrimp, peeled, deveined, and diced

4 oz. cooked crab, cleaned and diced

1 tablespoon shallots, minced

1 tablespoon chives, chopped

1 tablespoon fish sauce

2 tablespoons miso

1 tablespoon shrimp paste

2 tablespoons radish, chopped

1 tablespoon sesame seeds, toasted

1 teaspoon sesame oil

1 teaspoon sherry

12 wonton wrappers

For the Soup

1 tablespoon sesame oil

1 onion, finely chopped

2 carrots, peeled and finely chopped

2 garlic cloves, finely chopped

1 cup sake

4 cups fish stock (see page 20)

1 stalk lemongrass, bruised

1 tablespoon soy sauce

1 tablespoon fish sauce

Salt and pepper, to taste

1 romaine lettuce leaf, grated, for garnish

Toasted sesame seeds, for garnish

Cilantro, chopped, for garnish

Radish, shaved, for garnish

1 Begin by preparing the wontons. Combine all ingredients, save the wonton wrappers, in a bowl and mix until combined. Place 2 teaspoons of the mixture into the center of a wonton wrapper.

2 Dip your finger into cold water and rub a small amount around the edge of the wonton wrapper. Bring each corner together to make a purse and seal. Repeat with remaining wonton wrappers and refrigerate until ready to use.

3 To prepare the soup, add the sesame oil to a medium saucepan and cook over medium heat until warm. Add the onion and carrots and cook for 5 minutes, or until soft. Add the garlic, cook for 2 minutes, and then add the sake, fish stock, lemongrass, soy sauce, and fish sauce.

4 Simmer for 10 minutes, then remove the lemongrass and season the soup with salt and pepper. Bring the soup to a boil and add the wontons. Reduce heat so that the soup simmers and cook for 5 minutes, or until the wontons float to the top.

5 Place 3 wontons in each bowl. Ladle the broth over the wontons, and garnish with romaine lettuce, toasted sesame seeds, cilantro, and shaved radish.

Cullen Skink

The name of this soup originates from the town of Cullen in Northeast Scotland, a major fishing port back in its day.

INGREDIENTS

For the Bacon Jam

8 oz. thick-cut bacon

2 shallots, finely chopped

1 garlic clove, minced

2 tablespoons apple cider vinegar

2 tablespoons brown sugar

1 tablespoon maple syrup

For the Cullen Skink

9 oz. haddock fillet, skin on, smoked

1½ cups water

1 cup salt

4 cups milk, or enough to cover the haddock

4 tablespoons unsalted butter

1 onion, chopped

1 cup leeks, sliced

1 cup potato, peeled and chopped

Salt and pepper, to taste

Chives, chopped, for garnish

Crusty bread, to serve

1 Begin by preparing the Bacon Jam. Preheat oven to 350°F. Place the bacon in the oven and cook for 20 minutes, or until crispy. Reserve rendered fat. Finely chop the cooked bacon.

2 Place the reserved bacon fat in a medium saucepan and cook over medium heat until warm. Add shallots and garlic and cook for 5 minutes, or until translucent.

3 Add the apple cider vinegar, brown sugar, and maple syrup and simmer for 5 minutes. Add the chopped crispy bacon and let cool. Transfer to a container until ready to serve.

4 To prepare the Cullen Skink, add the haddock, water, and salt to a bowl and let stand for 10 minutes. Remove the haddock and rinse under cold water.

5 Place the haddock on a cooking rack with a tray underneath it. Lightly cover the tray and then place it in the refrigerator overnight.

6 Remove the haddock from the refrigerator and place it in a medium saucepan. Cover with the milk and simmer for 10 minutes, or until the fish becomes flaky. Remove the fish from the pan and reserve the poaching milk.

7 Meanwhile, in a medium saucepan, add the butter and cook over low heat until melted. Add the onion and cook for 5 minutes, or until soft.

8 Add the leeks, the potato, and the poaching milk to the saucepan and cook for 5 minutes, or until the potato is tender.

9 Use a fork to flake the haddock. Add flakes to the soup. Season with salt and pepper and ladle into warmed bowls. Garnish with chives and serve with Bacon Jam, and crusty bread.

Thai Fish Broth

This is a very fragrant broth thanks to the lemongrass, chilies, galangal root, lime juice, and lime leaf. It's meant to be very sour, which makes it perfect as a palate cleanser.

INGREDIENTS

4 cups fish stock (see page 20)

2 stalks of lemongrass, bruised with the back of a knife

Zest and juice of 2 limes

1-inch piece of galangal root, peeled and thinly sliced

6 stalks cilantro

1 kaffir lime leaf

2 monkfish fillets, skinned and cut into 1-inch pieces

12 small shrimp

2 Thai chilies, seeded and thinly sliced

1 tablespoon rice wine vinegar

4 tablespoons fish sauce

Cilantro leaves, chopped, for garnish

Bean sprouts, for garnish

Toasted sesame seeds, for garnish

Sesame oil, for garnish

1 In a medium saucepan, add the fish stock, lemongrass, lime zest, galangal root, cilantro stalks, and lime leaf and bring to a boil. Reduce the heat so that the broth simmers and cook for 5 minutes.

2 Turn off heat and let stand for 15 minutes. Strain the broth through a fine sieve. Return to a cleaned pan and bring to a boil.

3 Reduce heat so that the broth simmers. Add the lime juice, monkfish, shrimp, Thai chilies, rice wine vinegar, and fish sauce. Simmer for 3 to 4 minutes, or until the fish is cooked.

4 Ladle into warmed bowls and garnish with cilantro leaves, bean sprouts, toasted sesame seeds, and sesame oil.

Crab Veloute

The traditional technique for veloutes works perfectly with crab.

1 To make the Crispy Shallot Rings, add the shallots and the buttermilk to a bowl and let stand for 30 minutes. Place the oil in a Dutch oven and cook over medium heat until it is 350°F.

2 Combine the flour and cornstarch in a bowl and run through a fine sieve. Dredge the marinated shallots in the flour-and-cornstarch mixture. Drop each ring individually into the hot oil and fry until golden brown.

3 Remove from oil with tongs or a slotted spoon and set to drain on a paper towel. Season with salt and pepper and set aside.

4 To prepare the veloute, add the butter to a medium saucepan and cook over medium heat until melted. Add the shallots and cook for 3 minutes, or until soft.

5 Add the flour and cook for 3 minutes while stirring constantly. Add the stock, brandy, and tomato paste and stir until well-combined. Bring to a boil, reduce heat, and simmer for 10 minutes, or until the broth starts to thicken.

6 While simmering, prepare the Crab Bruschetta. Add the garlic, mayonnaise, anchovy, crab, and tarragon to a bowl and stir until well-combined. Season with salt and pepper. Spoon this mixture onto the bread, and garnish with a sprig of tarragon.

7 Remove the soup from heat and strain through a fine sieve. In a bowl, add the egg yolks and the cream and whisk until smooth.

8 Return the soup to the pan and bring to a simmer. Add $\frac{1}{3}$ cup of the hot soup to the egg-and-cream mixture. Whisk until combined and then add the egg mixture to the saucepan. Reduce heat to low and whisk constantly for 3 minutes.

9 Add the crab meat, lemon juice, cayenne pepper, salt, and pepper. Ladle into bowls and serve with Crab Bruschetta and Crispy Shallot Rings.

INGREDIENTS

For the Crispy Shallot Rings

2 shallots, finely sliced

⅓ cup of buttermilk

2 cups vegetable oil

¼ cup all-purpose flour

¼ cup cornstarch

Salt and pepper, to taste

For the Crab Veloute

2 tablespoons unsalted butter

2 shallots, chopped

2 tablespoons all-purpose flour

4 cups crab stock (see page 17)

⅛ cup brandy

2 tablespoons tomato paste

4 egg yolks

2 cups cream

2 cups crab meat, cooked, and chopped

1 teaspoon lemon juice

Pinch of cayenne pepper

Salt and pepper, to taste

For the Crab Bruschetta

½ garlic clove, minced

4 tablespoons mayonnaise

1 anchovy fillet, finely chopped

3 tablespoons crab meat, cooked

½ teaspoon tarragon, leaves removed and chopped, plus sprigs for garnish

Salt and pepper, to taste

4 slices of seeded bread, toasted

Chilled and Dessert Soups

When most people think of soup, this category doesn't pop into their heads. Sure, there are the classics like Vichyssoise, but there are a lot of other great options out there. On a warm summer's day, a chilled soup is a perfect appetizer or a hearty lunch. They are also perfect as a small amuse-bouche during a multi-course meal, teasing the palate before the real journey begins.

Chilled Pea Soup with Cheese Gougeres

YIELD: 4 TO 6 SERVINGS • ACTIVE TIME: 15 MINUTES
TOTAL TIME: 1 HOUR AND 15 MINUTES

This is a far cry from army-green split pea soup. Cooking the peas briefly retains their vibrant color, and the addition of spinach keeps the finished soup looking, and tasting, bright. Delicious warm or chilled, this one is guaranteed to become a springtime staple.

INGREDIENTS

For the Cheese Gougeres

¾ cup milk

¾ cup water

⅛ teaspoon salt

7 tablespoons unsalted butter

1¼ cups all-purpose flour

5 eggs, plus 1 egg for egg wash

1¼ cups Gruyère cheese, grated

2 tablespoons water

For the Chilled Pea Soup

1 tablespoon extra virgin olive oil

½ onion, peeled and diced

1 sprig mint

4 cups vegetable stock (see page 25)

3 lbs. peas, frozen

4 cups spinach

Salt and pepper, to taste

1 To make the Cheese Gougers, preheat oven to 400°F. In a medium saucepan, add the milk, water, salt, and butter and bring to a boil. Add the flour and stir constantly until a ball of dough forms.

2 Remove dough from pan and place in a standing mixer. Mix slowly until the dough stops steaming. Add the 5 eggs one at a time. Add the cheese and mix until combined.

3 Line a baking tray with a baking mat or parchment paper and spoon the dough onto it.

4 In a small bowl, add the remaining egg and the water and whisk until combined. Brush this wash on top of dough and place tray in oven. Bake for 20 minutes, or until golden brown, then remove and let cool on a wire rack.

5 To make the soup, add the olive oil and onions to a medium saucepan and cook over medium heat for 5 minutes, or until the onions are soft. Add the mint sprig and stir.

6 After 1 minute, add the stock and bring to a boil. Remove from heat and add the frozen peas. Transfer the soup to a food processor, add the spinach, and puree until smooth.

7 Strain through a fine sieve, season with salt and pepper, and serve with Cheese Gougeres.

Red Bell Pepper Soup with Sambuca Cream

YIELD: 6 SERVINGS • ACTIVE TIME: 25 MINUTES • TOTAL TIME: 55 MINUTES

Take the Sambuca out from behind the bar and bring it into the kitchen. Once mixed in, the Sambuca Cream brings out the flavors of the fennel seed, herbs, and jalapeño.

1 To make the soup, add half the oil to a medium saucepan and cook over medium heat until warm. Add the onion, fennel seed, thyme, bay leaf, garlic, basil, and jalapeño, reduce heat to low, and cook for 5 minutes, or until the onion is soft.

2 Add the flour and cook, while stirring constantly, for 5 minutes. Add the stock, tomato, and tomato paste and bring to a boil.

3 Meanwhile, in a large sauté pan, add the remaining oil and the red bell peppers. Cook over medium until the peppers blister and char slightly. Add the peppers to the soup and cook, while stirring occasionally, for 20 minutes.

4 Transfer the soup to a food processor, puree until smooth and creamy, and pass through a fine sieve.

5 Return the pureed soup to the pan, bring to a simmer, and add the cream and sugar. Season with salt and pepper.

6 Prepare the Sambuca Cream by placing cream in a bowl and whisking until soft peaks form. Add the remaining ingredients to the bowl, whisk until soft peaks form, and set aside.

7 Just before serving, add the Sambuca to the soup. Ladle into bowls, serve with Sambuca Cream, and garnish with basil.

INGREDIENTS

For the Red Bell Pepper Soup

¾ cup extra virgin olive oil

1 cup onion, chopped

1 tablespoon fennel seed

¼ teaspoon thyme, leaves removed and chopped

1 bay leaf

½ teaspoon garlic, minced

1 tablespoon basil, chopped, plus more for garnish

1 tablespoon jalapeño, stem and seeds removed, diced

¼ cup all-purpose flour

5 cups chicken stock (see page 14)

½ cup tomato, concasse (see page 117) and chopped

1 teaspoon tomato paste

6 large red bell peppers, halved, seeded, and chopped

1 cup heavy cream

Pinch of sugar

Salt and pepper, to taste

4 tablespoons Sambuca

For the Sambuca Cream

½ cup heavy cream

¼ teaspoon lemon juice

⅛ teaspoon lemon zest

2 tablespoons Sambuca

Fontina Cheese Soup in a Sourdough Bread Bowl

YIELDS: 4 SERVINGS • ACTIVE TIME: 30 MINUTES • TOTAL TIME: 1 HOUR

This delicious, cheesy soup absorbs nicely into the bread and allows you to eat your "bowl" when you finish. You might argue that the leftover soaked bread is even better than the soup.

INGREDIENTS

½ cup unsalted butter

2 onions, chopped

2 sprigs thyme, leaves removed and chopped

4 tablespoons all-purpose flour

4 cups chicken stock (see page 14)

4 cups milk

8 cups fontina cheese, grated

Salt and pepper

4 sourdough bread rolls or 1 large boule

Chives, to garnish

1 In a medium saucepan on medium heat, melt the butter.

2 Add the onion and thyme and cook for 5 minutes or until soft. Then, add the flour and cook for 5 minutes. Add the chicken stock and milk and bring to a boil.

3 Remove the pan from heat, add the cheese, and whisk until combined.

4 In a food processor, blend the soup until smooth and strain through a fine sieve. Return to a clean pan and season with salt and pepper.

5 With a small serrated knife, remove the tops of the sourdough bread, remove the innards, and toast. Pour the soup in the middle and garnish with chives.

Vichyssoise

Vichyssoise is traditionally served cold, but it can be eaten hot.

INGREDIENTS

For the Chive Oil

4 cups of water

1 cup chives, chopped

1 cup baby spinach

1 cup vegetable oil

For the Simple Croutons

Sliced brioche, cut into
¼-inch cubes

1 tablespoon extra virgin
olive oil

Salt and pepper, to taste

For the Vichyssoise

4 tablespoons unsalted
butter

6 leeks, white part only,
thinly sliced

3 large shallots, chopped

1 Idaho potato, peeled
and cubed

6 cups chicken stock
(see page 14)

Salt and pepper, to taste

Pinch of nutmeg

1 cup heavy cream

1 To prepare the Chive Oil, bring the water to a boil in a small saucepan. Add the chives and spinach, cook for 1 minute, remove, and submerge in ice water. Remove from ice water and squeeze out any excess water.

2 In a food processor, add the chives, spinach, and the oil. Puree for 3 to 4 minutes, strain through cheesecloth, and reserve until ready to use.

3 To make the Simple Croutons, preheat the oven to 350°F. Spread the brioche out on a baking tray. Drizzle with olive oil and bake for 5 minutes, or until golden brown. Remove, season with salt and pepper, and set on a paper towel to cool.

4 To make the soup, add the butter to a medium saucepan and cook over medium heat until warm. Add the leeks and shallots and cook for 5 minutes, or until soft. Add the potato and cook for 3 minutes. Transfer to a food processor, puree until creamy, and strain through a fine sieve.

5 Add the chicken stock and bring to a boil. Reduce to a simmer, partially cover the pan, and cook until the potato is soft.

6 Season with salt, pepper, and nutmeg. Add the heavy cream and place the soup in the refrigerator to chill. Serve in chilled bowls with Chive Oil and Simple Croutons.

Golden Gazpacho with Grilled Cheese

YIELD: 4 TO 6 SERVINGS • ACTIVE TIME: 30 MINUTES • TOTAL TIME: 2½ HOURS

If you love Gazpacho, try this spectacular version that is a twist on the classic. Using only yellow vegetables gives it its special color and transforms the flavor.

INGREDIENTS

For the Golden Gazpacho

6 ears of corn, kernels removed

9 golden tomatoes, chopped

2 yellow bell peppers, seeds removed and chopped

1 onion, chopped

3 garlic cloves, minced

½ cup extra virgin olive oil

4 tablespoons apple cider vinegar

Salt and pepper, to taste

Parsley, chopped, for garnish

For the Grilled Cheese

½ cup unsalted butter, softened

8 to 12 slices brioche

2 to 3 cups fontina cheese, grated

1 To make the gazpacho, combine all the ingredients in a mixing bowl and let chill in refrigerator for at least 30 minutes and up to 1 hour.

2 Transfer the soup to a food processor, blend until smooth, and strain through a fine sieve. Season with salt and pepper, return to refrigerator, and chill for at least 1 hour.

3 While the soup chills, prepare the Grilled Cheese. Preheat the oven to 350°F. Spread the softened butter on each slice of brioche. Sprinkle the cheese on the non-buttered sides of the bread. Make sandwiches out of the pieces of bread.

4 Place a large sauté pan over medium heat and add the sandwiches to the pan. Cook until golden brown, flip, and repeat on the other side.

5 Keep the sandwiches on the pan and place in the oven for 5 minutes, or until heated through. Remove from oven, cut in half, and serve.

6 Ladle the soup into chilled bowls, garnish with parsley, and serve with Grilled Cheese.

Chilled Watermelon and Cherry Soup with Watermelon Ice Cubes

YIELD: 4 SERVINGS • ACTIVE TIME: 20 MINUTES • TOTAL TIME: 9½ HOURS

This makes for a great intermezzo or amuse-bouche. The ice cubes keep the soup chilled without watering it down.

INGREDIENTS

For the Watermelon Ice Cubes

1 cup watermelon, cut into ½-inch cubes

1 tablespoon kirsch

Zest and juice of 1 lime

½ vanilla bean, seeds scraped and pod reserved

For the Chilled Watermelon and Cherry Soup

1½ cups watermelon, peeled and chopped

¾ cup cherries, pitted, fresh or frozen

1 cup Riesling

1 cup Champagne

1 To make the Watermelon Ice Cubes, combine all ingredients in a bowl and chill in the refrigerator for 1 hour. Transfer to a baking tray and freeze overnight. Cut into cubes and serve

2 To make the soup, add the watermelon, cherries, and Riesling to a food processor and puree until smooth. Strain through a fine sieve and chill in the refrigerator.

3 Right before serving, add the Champagne and Watermelon Ice Cubes to the soup. Serve in chilled glasses.

Hungarian Cherry Soup with Roasted Vanilla Cherries

YIELD: 4 SERVINGS • ACTIVE TIME: 20 MINUTES • TOTAL TIME: 9½ HOURS

In Central Europe, seasonal fruits are often employed in soup—a great way to celebrate ingredients at their freshest. The demerara sugar provides a great smoky flavor. If using fresh cherries, it's important to pit them after roasting, as this will allow the cherries to hold their shape.

INGREDIENTS

For the Roasted Vanilla Cherries

24 cherries

2 tablespoons demerara sugar

Pinch of sea salt

¼ cup brandy

½ vanilla bean, scraped

For the Hungarian Cherry Soup

1¼ lbs. cherries, halved and pitted

¾ cup water

¾ cup sugar

1 cinnamon stick

2 cups red wine

¾ cup sour cream, plus more for garnish

¼ cup milk

¼ cup heavy cream

1 To make the Roasted Vanilla Cherries, combine all the ingredients in a bowl and place in the refrigerator to marinate overnight.

2 Preheat oven to 400°F. Pass the contents of the bowl through a fine sieve. Place the cherries on a baking tray and reserve the liquid.

3 Place cherries in the oven for 5 minutes. Remove and carefully add half of the liquid. Stir gently and return to oven for 5 minutes.

4 Remove from oven, add the remaining liquid, and stir gently. Return to oven for 5 more minutes, remove from oven, and chill in the refrigerator. When chilled, pit the cherries and set aside.

5 To prepare the soup, combine cherries, water, sugar, cinnamon stick, and red wine in a large saucepan. Bring to a boil, then reduce heat so the mixture simmers. Cook for 20 minutes.

6 Transfer the soup to a food processor and puree. Transfer the pureed soup to a container and chill in the refrigerator.

7 When the soup is chilled, add the sour cream to a bowl and then slowly add the milk and heavy cream. Stir until it has a smooth consistency.

8 Combine the chilled cherry puree and the sour cream mixture by hand. Return to the refrigerator and chill until ready to serve. Ladle into chilled bowls, garnish with sour cream, and serve with Roasted Vanilla Cherries.

Chilled Mango, Coconut, and Curry Soup

YIELD: 4 TO 6 SERVINGS • ACTIVE TIME: 15 MINUTES • TOTAL TIME: 30 MINUTES

Don't be scared about the curry—the flavor is very mild and refreshing.

1 Combine all ingredients for the soup in a food processor and blend until it has a soupy consistency. Pass through a fine sieve.

2 To prepare the Coconut Froth, place all ingredients in a bowl and use a hand blender to combine. Blend until frothy.

3 Serve the soup in chilled bowls or glasses, and top with Coconut Froth.

INGREDIENTS

For the Chilled Mango, Coconut, and Curry Soup

3 cups ripe mango, peeled and chopped

3 (14 oz.) cans coconut milk

4 teaspoons curry powder

For the Coconut Froth

½ cup coconut milk

½ cup milk

1 tablespoon heavy cream

1 tablespoon sugar

Coconut and Tapioca Soup with Mint-Infused Mango

YIELD: 4 TO 6 SERVINGS • ACTIVE TIME: 30 MINUTES • TOTAL TIME: 3½ HOURS

Tapioca is not seen much these days, but it was very popular back in the '80s. This soup is worth starting a tapioca resurgence for sure.

INGREDIENTS

For the Mint-Infused Mango

½ cup water

½ cup white wine

½ cup sugar

Zest of 1 lime

2 sprigs mint, leaves removed and chopped

1 cup mango, cubed

For the Coconut Tuile

⅓ cup unsweeteed coconut, grated

¼ cup powdered sugar

1 tablespoon all-purpose flour

1 tablespoon unsalted butter, melted

1 egg white

For the Coconut and Tapioca Soup

5 cups milk, plus more if necessary

½ cup sugar

1 vanilla bean, halved and scraped

1 cup small tapioca pearls

1 (14 oz.) can of coconut milk

Mint leaves, for garnish

1 To prepare the Mint-Infused Mango, add the water, white wine, sugar, and lime zest to a small saucepan and bring to a boil. Remove from heat, add the mint sprigs, and cover. Let stand until cool.

2 Once cool, place in a bowl with the mango and let chill in refrigerator for at least 2 hours before serving.

3 To prepare the Coconut Tuile, in a mixing bowl, combine the coconut, powdered sugar, and flour and combine with a whisk.

4 In a separate bowl, add the melted butter and the egg white and whisk vigorously until combined.

5 Add the coconut mixture to the butter-and-egg mixture and combine. Chill in refrigerator for 2 hours.

6 Preheat oven to 350°F. Spread the chilled tuile on baking mat and then place on a baking tray. Place the tray in the oven and cook for 8 minutes, or until golden brown.

7 To make the soup, add the milk, sugar, vanilla seeds, and vanilla pod to a large saucepan and bring to a boil. Reduce heat so that the soup simmers and add the tapioca pearls. Cook for 10 minutes, or until the tapioca pearls are soft.

8 Remove pan from heat, add coconut milk, and let stand until cool. Serve in a chilled glass, or return to a simmer (adjusting consistency with more milk, if necessary) and ladle into warm bowls.

9 Serve with Coconut Tuile and Mint-Infused Mango and garnish with mint leaves.

Soups for Kids

This chapter doesn't just have smaller versions or stereotypical choices—these soups are geared toward children's whimsical (if picky) appetites. If your kids are fans of chicken nuggets and mac and cheese and pretty much nothing else, you'll be surprised how quickly they'll change their minds with these fun recipes.

Broccoli Soup

YIELD: 4 SERVINGS • ACTIVE TIME: 10 MINUTES • TOTAL TIME: 30 MINUTES

This very healthy and quick soup just may get your kids to eat their vegetables.

INGREDIENTS

¼ cup unsalted butter

1 onion, peeled and diced

2 celery stalks, chopped

2 garlic cloves

2 carrots, peeled and chopped

1½ lbs. broccoli florets

4 cups chicken stock (see page 14)

Salt and pepper, to taste

Cheddar cheese, grated, for garnish

1 In a medium saucepan, add the butter and cook over medium heat until it is melted.

2 Add the onion, celery, garlic, and carrots and cook for 5 minutes, or until soft.

3 Add the broccoli and chicken stock and bring to a boil.

4 Reduce heat so that the soup simmers. Cook for 10 minutes, or until the broccoli is soft.

5 Transfer the soup to a food processor and puree until smooth.

6 Return to a clean pan. Bring to a simmer and season with salt and pepper.

7 Serve in bowls garnished with grated cheddar cheese.

Baked Potato Soup

YIELD: 4 SERVINGS • ACTIVE TIME: 20 MINUTES • TOTAL TIME: 1½ HOURS

Based off the classic baked potato, this is a soup your kids will absolutely love. Garnishing the soup with chopped bacon gives it a very authentic taste and texture.

1 Preheat oven to 400°F. Use a fork to pierce the potatoes. Place them on a baking tray and bake for 1 hour, or until tender.

2 When potatoes are cooked, remove from oven and allow them to cool slightly. Peel and mash with a fork.

3 Meanwhile, in a medium saucepan add the butter and cook over medium heat until it is melted. Add the flour and stir until combined.

4 Add the milk and bring soup to a simmer, while stirring constantly. Cook for 5 minutes, or until the soup thickens.

5 Add the mashed potatoes and half of the cheese. Stir until the cheese melts. Remove the pan from heat and stir in the sour cream.

6 Season with salt and pepper and serve in bowls garnished with the remaining cheese, scallions, and the bacon.

INGREDIENTS

2 large Idaho potatoes

¼ cup unsalted butter

⅓ cup all-purpose flour

4 cups milk

1½ cups sharp cheddar cheese, grated

½ cup sour cream

Salt and pepper, to taste

⅔ cup scallions, chopped, for garnish

8 slices thick-cut bacon, cooked and chopped, for garnish

Chilled Peanut Butter and Jelly Soup

YIELD: 4 CHILD-SIZED SERVINGS • ACTIVE TIME: 15 MINUTES
TOTAL TIME: 1 HOUR AND 15 MINUTES

Who doesn't love a peanut butter and jelly sandwich? How about a chilled version as a soup? Make each soup separately, chill, and then combine in a chilled bowl. It's guaranteed to wow anyone.

INGREDIENTS

For the Strawberry Soup

2 cups strawberries, greens removed and chopped, plus more for garnish

1½ cups Greek yogurt

Juice of 1 lime

1 teaspoon salt

1 cup confectioners' sugar, sieved

¼ cup heavy cream

For the Peanut Soup

2 tablespoons unsalted butter

1 celery stalk, chopped

½ onion, chopped

1 tablespoon all-purpose flour

2 cups chicken stock (see page 14)

½ cup milk

½ cup peanut butter

1 To make the Strawberry Soup, combine all ingredients in a food processor and puree until smooth. Place in the refrigerator and chill for 1 hour.

2 To make the Peanut Soup, add the butter to a small saucepan and cook over medium heat until it is melted. Add the celery and onion and cook for 3 minutes, or until soft. Add the flour and cook for 2 minutes.

3 Slowly add the chicken stock and milk to the pan. Let soup simmer for 5 minutes, or until it has thickened. Transfer the soup to a food processor and blend until smooth.

4 Return to the pan and add the peanut butter. Whisk until combined and then chill in the refrigerator for 1 hour. Once chilled, combine both soups into chilled bowls, garnish with strawberry halves, and serve.

Lasagna Soup

This warm, rich soup is great for a birthday party, or when your children's friends come over to play.

1 Cook the lasagna noodles according to manufacturer's instructions. Drain and set aside.

2 In a medium saucepan, add the olive oil and cook over medium heat until warm.

3 Add the onion and cook for 5 minutes, or until soft.

4 Add the sausage, garlic, and oregano and cook for about 3 minutes, or until sausage is browned. Break the sausage up with a wooden spoon so it cooks evenly.

5 Add the tomato paste, beef stock, and tomatoes and bring to a boil.

6 Reduce heat so that the soup simmers and cook for 10 minutes.

7 Stir in the noodles, basil, Parmesan, and heavy cream. Simmer for 2 minutes to melt the cheese.

8 Serve in bowls garnished with ricotta and basil.

INGREDIENTS

12 lasagna noodles, broken into pieces

2 tablespoons extra virgin olive oil

1 onion, peeled and chopped

1 lb. ground Italian sausage

2 garlic cloves, minced

2 teaspoons dried oregano

2 tablespoons tomato paste

4 cups beef stock (see page 12)

2 (14 oz.) cans crushed tomatoes

½ cup basil, chopped, reserve some for garnish

¼ cup Parmesan cheese, grated

¼ cup heavy cream

1 cup ricotta cheese, for garnish

Macaroni and Cheese Soup

YIELD: 4 SERVINGS • ACTIVE TIME: 15 MINUTES • TOTAL TIME: 40 MINUTES

Turn this children's classic into a soup and you're sure to be the favorite chef.

INGREDIENTS

1½ cups elbow pasta

¼ cup unsalted butter

1 onion, peeled and chopped

2 carrots, peeled and chopped

2 celery stalks, chopped

2 tablespoons all-purpose flour

4 cups chicken stock (see page 14)

2 cups milk

4 cups sharp cheddar cheese, grated

Salt and pepper, to taste

1 Cook the pasta according to the manufacturer's instructions. Drain and set aside.

2 In a medium saucepan, add the butter and cook over low heat until melted.

3 Add the onion, carrots, and celery. Stirring frequently, cook for 5 minutes, or until the vegetables are soft.

4 Add the flour and cook for 5 minutes.

5 Add the chicken stock and milk and bring to a boil. Reduce heat so that the soup simmers and cook for 10 minutes.

6 Remove pan from heat and add the grated cheddar cheese. Mix together with a whisk.

7 Season with salt and pepper, add cooked pasta, and serve.

Purple Cauliflower Soup

YIELD: 4 SERVINGS • ACTIVE TIME: 15 MINUTES • TOTAL TIME: 45 MINUTES

Who says food can't look fun? This beautiful purple soup is certain to look inviting to your children.

1 In a medium saucepan, add the butter and cook over medium heat until melted.

2 Add the onions, chopped cauliflower, and beets and cook for 5 minutes or until soft.

3 Add the stock and bring to a boil.

4 Reduce the heat so that the soup simmers and cook for 5 minutes.

5 Add the cream and simmer for 10 minutes.

6 Transfer the soup to a food processor and puree until creamy. Strain through a fine sieve, return to a clean pan, and bring to a simmer.

7 Season to taste, serve in warmed bowls, and garnish with Parmesan.

INGREDIENTS

¼ cup unsalted butter

1 onion, peeled and diced

1 purple cauliflower, florets removed from stem and chopped

½ cup beets, peeled and chopped

4 cups vegetable stock (see page 25)

2 cups heavy cream

Salt and pepper, to taste

½ cup Parmesan cheese, grated, for garnish

Vegetable Minestrone

YIELD: 4 SERVINGS • ACTIVE TIME: 20 MINUTES • TOTAL TIME: 1 HOUR

This is a healthy vegetable soup that is perfect for kids, who will be drawn to the orzo and the Parmesan.

INGREDIENTS

2 tablespoons extra virgin olive oil

1 onion, chopped

1 leek, chopped

2 celery stalks, chopped

2 carrots, peeled and chopped

2 (14 oz.) cans diced tomatoes

2 garlic cloves, minced

4 cups vegetable stock (see page 25)

2 cups green cabbage, chopped

2 teaspoons oregano, chopped

1 bay leaf

¼ cup tomato paste

½ cup orzo

Salt and pepper, to taste

½ cup Parmesan cheese, grated, for garnish

1 In a medium saucepan, add the olive oil and cook over medium heat until warm. Add the onion, leek, celery, and carrots and cook for 5 minutes, or until soft.

2 Stir in the tomatoes and garlic and simmer for 10 minutes. Add the vegetable stock, cabbage, oregano, bay leaf, and tomato paste.

3 Bring to a boil, reduce heat so that the soup simmers, and cook for 10 minutes. Add the orzo and cook for 10 minutes, or until pasta is al dente.

4 Season with salt and pepper, ladle into warm bowls, and garnish with grated Parmesan.

Taco Soup

YIELD: 4 SERVINGS • ACTIVE TIME: 20 MINUTES • TOTAL TIME: 45 MINUTES

Tacos are great, but they can be messy. Cut down on your cleanup time by tossing everything into this one-pot soup.

INGREDIENTS

2 tablespoons vegetable oil

1 onion, chopped

1 red bell pepper, seeds removed and chopped

1 green bell pepper, seeds removed and chopped

1 lb. ground beef

2 tablespoons taco seasoning

2 cups beef stock (see page 12)

2 cups spaghetti sauce

2 (14 oz.) cans diced tomatoes

2 cups cooked black beans

2 cups cooked kidney beans

2 cups cooked corn kernels

½ cup salsa

4 cups tortilla chips, for garnish

2 cups Monterey Jack cheese, grated, for garnish

1 cup sour cream, for garnish

1 In a medium saucepan, add the oil and cook over medium heat until warm. Add the onion and bell peppers and cook for 5 minutes, or until soft.

2 Add the ground beef and taco seasoning and cook for 5 minutes. Add the beef stock, spaghetti sauce, and diced tomatoes and bring to a simmer. Cook for 10 minutes.

3 Add the black beans, kidney beans, and corn kernels. Return to a simmer, add salsa, and simmer for 5 additional minutes.

4 Serve in bowls, and garnish with tortilla chips, Monterey Jack cheese, and sour cream.

Tomato Alphabet Soup

YIELD: 4 SERVINGS • ACTIVE TIME: 15 MINUTES • TOTAL TIME: 45 MINUTES

This is not just a tasty soup, it's also fun. You could also serve the letters separately and let the kids practice the alphabet.

INGREDIENTS

1 cup alphabet pasta

¼ cup unsalted butter

2 onions, chopped

4 carrots, peeled and chopped

2 celery stalks, chopped

3 cups vegetable stock (see page 25)

2 teaspoons basil, chopped

4 (14 oz.) cans diced tomatoes

Salt and pepper, to taste

1 Cook the pasta according to the manufacturer's instructions. Drain and set aside.

2 In a medium saucepan, add the butter and cook over medium heat until melted.

3 Add the onions, carrots, and celery and cook for 5 minutes, or until soft.

4 Add the vegetable stock, basil, and tomatoes and bring to a boil.

5 Reduce heat so that the soup simmers and cook for 10 minutes.

6 Transfer soup to a food processor and puree until smooth.

7 Return to a clean pan, bring to a simmer, and add the cooked pasta. Season with salt and pepper and serve in warmed bowls.

Wagon Wheel Beef Soup

YIELD: 4 SERVINGS • ACTIVE TIME: 15 MINUTES • TOTAL TIME: 40 MINUTES

A great, comforting soup that is easy to prepare. Your children will get a healthy meal, all while having fun with the wagon wheels. Feel free to add other types of ground meat or switch the kidney beans out for other legumes or vegetables that they like.

1 Cook pasta according to manufacturer's instructions. Drain and set aside.

2 In a medium saucepan, add the vegetable oil and cook over medium heat until warm. Add onions and cook for 5 minutes, or until soft.

3 Add the ground beef and cook for an additional 5 minutes.

4 Add the spaghetti sauce, oregano, beef stock, and kidney beans and bring to a gentle simmer. Cook for 10 minutes.

5 Add the cooked pasta, season with salt and pepper, and serve in warmed bowls.

INGREDIENTS

1 cup wagon wheel pasta

2 tablespoons vegetable oil

1 cup onion, chopped

1 lb. ground beef

4 cups spaghetti sauce

½ teaspoon ground oregano

2 cups beef stock (see page 12)

2 cups kidney beans, drained and cooked

Salt and pepper, to taste

30 Minutes or Less

The secret to a lot of great soups is time, but this chapter touches on a few soups that you can whip up quickly. Bear in mind, having a well-developed stock on hand is a big help for these quick preparations, as it will be tasked with providing a lot of the soup's flavor. To cut down on cooking time, these recipes use a couple handy tricks, such as grating the vegetables and using tender cuts of meat.

Bouillabaisse

YIELD: 4 SERVINGS • ACTIVE TIME: 20 MINUTES • TOTAL TIME: 30 MINUTES

Prepare all your ingredients in advance so that once your guests arrive you can quickly put together this classic.

1 Preheat oven to 200°F. Place four bowls in the oven. In a medium saucepan, add 1 tablespoon of the oil and the lobster tails, flesh-side down. Cook over medium heat.

2 Add the clams and cook for 2 minutes. Add the mussels, lobster stock, orange zest, orange juice, and saffron, cover, and cook for 5 minutes, or until the clams and mussels are open. Discard any that do not open.

3 In a medium sauté pan, add 1 tablespoon of the vegetable oil and the shrimp, and cook over medium heat. Cook the shrimp for 2 minutes on each side.

4 Add the shrimp to the broth in the saucepan, cover, and cook for an additional 2 minutes. Remove the shellfish with a slotted spoon and place in four warmed bowls in the oven.

5 Strain the broth through a fine sieve and then return to the pan. Simmer until it is reduced by half. Place the sole in a mixing bowl and gently combine it with the flour, until both sides of each piece are coated.

6 Gently tap the fish to remove any excess flour, season with salt and pepper, and place in a medium sauté pan with the remaining oil. Cook for 2 minutes on each side.

7 When the stock has reduced, add the butter to the broth slowly, whisking constantly. Season the broth with salt and pepper.

8 Remove the warmed bowls from the oven, pour the broth over the seafood, and then add the cooked sole. Garnish with chopped parsley, and serve with crusty bread.

INGREDIENTS

4 tablespoons
vegetable oil

2 whole raw lobster
tails, cut in half in
the shell and rinsed

16 clams

24 mussels

4 cups lobster stock
(see page 23)

Zest and juice
of 1 orange

⅛ teaspoon saffron

16 shrimp, cleaned

1 lb. Dover sole,
skin removed and cut
into 2-inch pieces

¼ cup all-purpose flour

Salt and pepper, to taste

½ cup unsalted butter,
cut into small pieces
and chilled

2 tablespoons parsley,
chopped, for garnish

Crusty bread, to serve

Acorn Squash Soup with Fennel Salad

YIELD: 4 SERVINGS • ACTIVE TIME: 15 MINUTES • TOTAL TIME: 30 MINUTES

Serve this fall-flavored soup with a refreshing fennel salad.

INGREDIENTS

For the Fennel Salad

½ fennel bulb, outer layer removed, sliced thin

Zest and juice of 1 orange

1 tablespoon Pernod

2 tablespoons extra virgin olive oil

2 tablespoons fennel fronds

1 tablespoon fennel pollen

Salt and pepper, to taste

For the Acorn Squash Soup

1 tablespoon vegetable oil

8 slices of thick-cut bacon, chopped

2 acorn squash, peeled, halved, seeds removed, and grated

1 onion, peeled and chopped

2 apples, peeled and grated

1 teaspoon five-spice powder

¼ teaspoon cayenne pepper

4 cups chicken stock (see page 14)

2 cups heavy cream

Salt and pepper, to taste

1 To make the Fennel Salad, place the fennel slices in a serving bowl. Add the remaining ingredients and toss gently. Season with salt and pepper and set aside until the soup is done.

2 To make the soup, add the vegetable oil to a medium saucepan and cook over medium heat. Add the bacon and cook for 5 minutes, or until crispy. Use a slotted spoon to remove the bacon from the pan. Set to drain on a paper towel. Reserve ¼ cup for garnish.

3 Add the acorn squash and onion to the pan and cook for 5 minutes, or until soft. Add the remaining bacon, apples, five-spice powder, cayenne pepper, and chicken stock and bring to a boil.

4 Reduce heat so that the soup simmers and cook for 10 minutes. Remove the soup from the pot. Transfer to a food processor, puree until smooth, and strain through a fine sieve.

5 Return the soup to a clean pan and bring to a simmer. Add the heavy cream and cook for 5 minutes.

6 Season with salt and pepper and serve in warmed bowls with the reserved bacon and Fennel Salad.

Chilled Honeydew Melon Soup with Crispy Prosciutto di Parma

YIELD: 4 SERVINGS • ACTIVE TIME: 15 MINUTES • TOTAL TIME: 30 MINUTES

A refreshing, classical preparation of melon and prosciutto, all in no time flat.

INGREDIENTS

For the Chilled Honeydew Melon Soup

1 honeydew melon, peeled, halved, seeds removed

1 tablespoon lemon juice

2 cups dry white wine, chilled

⅛ cup sugar

Fresh grapes, for garnish

Lemon zest, for garnish

For the Crispy Prosciutto di Parma

8 slices prosciutto

1 To make the soup, puree the melon and lemon juice in a food processor and then strain through a fine sieve. Chill in the refrigerator for 20 minutes.

2 While the soup chills, prepare the Crispy Prosciutto di Parma. Preheat oven to 375°F. Line a baking tray with a baking mat or parchment paper and place the slices of prosciutto on the tray.

3 When oven is preheated, place tray in oven and bake for 5 to 10 minutes, or until the prosciutto is crispy. Remove tray from oven and place prosciutto on a paper towel to drain.

4 Just before serving the soup, add the chilled white wine, whisk until combined, and then season with just enough sugar to emphasize the melon flavor.

5 Ladle into chilled bowls, serve with Crispy Prosciutto di Parma, and garnish with fresh grapes and lemon zest.

Cream of Broccoli Soup

YIELD: 4 SERVINGS • ACTIVE TIME: 15 MINUTES • TOTAL TIME: 30 MINUTES

It seems criminal that such a wonderful trip back to the past can be ready in 30 minutes.

INGREDIENTS

2 tablespoons unsalted butter

1 tablespoon extra virgin olive oil

1 onion, diced

1 crown of broccoli, florets removed and chopped

1 sprig thyme, leaves removed and chopped

1 sprig rosemary, leaves removed and chopped

4 cups chicken or vegetable stock (see page 14 or 25)

2 cups heavy cream

Salt and pepper, to taste

1 In a medium saucepan, add the butter and olive oil and cook over medium heat until the butter is melted.

2 Add the onion and cook for 5 minutes, or until soft. Add the broccoli and herbs and cook for an additional 3 minutes.

3 Add the stock and bring to a boil. Reduce the flame so that the soup simmers and cook for 5 minutes.

4 Add the heavy cream and simmer for 10 minutes, or until the broccoli is tender.

5 Remove pan from heat and transfer soup to a food processor. Puree until the soup is creamy.

6 Return the soup to a clean pan, bring to a simmer, and season with salt and pepper. Serve in warmed bowls.

Fast Pho

YIELD: 4 SERVINGS • ACTIVE TIME: 15 MINUTES • TOTAL TIME: 30 MINUTES

All this in just 30 minutes? That can't be pho real.

1 In a medium saucepan, add the oil and cook over medium heat until warm. Add the onion and ginger and cook for 5 minutes, or until soft.

2 Meanwhile, in a sauté pan, add the spices and cook over medium heat for 2 to 3 minutes, until they become fragrant. Add to the saucepan.

3 Add the beef stock and bring to a boil. Reduce heat so broth simmers and cook for 10 minutes.

4 Strain the soup into a clean pot. Season with fish sauce, hoisin, and Sriracha and return to a simmer.

5 Place the rice noodles into a bowl and cover with boiling water. Leave to soak for 4 minutes, or according to manufacturer's instructions.

6 Combine rice noodles and soup in warm bowls. Garnish with sliced jalapeño, bean sprouts, lime wedges, and Thai basil and serve.

INGREDIENTS

2 tablespoons vegetable oil

1 small yellow onion, peeled and chopped

1-inch piece ginger, peeled

2 cinnamon sticks

3 star anise

2 cardamom pods, seeds removed and chopped

1 cup cilantro

5 cloves

1 tablespoon coriander seed

1 tablespoon fennel seed

1 tablespoon black peppercorns

6 cups beef stock (see page 12)

1 tablespoon fish sauce

1 tablespoon hoisin

1 teaspoon Sriracha

3 oz. rice noodles

1 jalapeño, sliced, for garnish

Bean Sprouts, for garnish

Lime wedges, for garnish

Thai basil, for garnish

Cream of Tomato Soup with Sourdough Garlic Bread

YIELD: 4 SERVINGS • ACTIVE TIME: 20 MINUTES • TOTAL TIME: 30 MINUTES

A quick, classic soup served with its favorite partner: garlic bread. Perfect for those nights when you need to simplify.

INGREDIENTS

For the Sourdough Garlic Bread

1 cup unsalted butter, softened

1½ teaspoons lemon juice

2 garlic cloves, minced

3 tablespoons parsley, chopped

Salt and pepper, to taste

8 slices sourdough bread

For the Cream of Tomato Soup

2 tablespoons unsalted butter

1 onion, chopped

2 (14 oz.) cans stewed tomatoes

2 carrots, peeled and grated

5 cups chicken stock (see page 14)

2 tablespoons parsley, chopped

½ teaspoon thyme, chopped

6 tablespoons heavy cream

Salt and pepper, to taste

Parmesan cheese, grated, for garnish

1 To make the Sourdough Garlic Bread, preheat oven to 425°F. In a bowl, whisk the butter for 2 minutes by hand in order to lighten it. Add the remaining ingredients, except the bread, to the bowl, season with salt and pepper, and combine.

2 Spread the butter on each slice of bread. Make 2 stacks of buttered bread and wrap each in aluminum foil. Place in oven for 10 to 15 minutes, until the butter is melted and the edges are crispy.

3 To make the soup, add the butter to a large saucepan and cook over medium heat until melted. Add the onion and cook for 5 minutes, or until soft.

4 Stir in the tomatoes, carrots, chicken stock, parsley, and thyme and bring to a boil. Reduce to a simmer and cook for 10 minutes, or until the vegetables are tender.

5 Remove soup from heat and transfer to a food processor. Puree the soup and pass through a fine sieve.

6 Return the soup to the pan and add the cream. Reheat and season with salt and pepper. Serve with Sourdough Garlic Bread and garnish with Parmesan.

Creamed Parsnip Soup with Arugula Pesto

YIELD: 4 SERVINGS • ACTIVE TIME: 15 MINUTES • TOTAL TIME: 30 MINUTES

Grating the parsnips speeds up the cooking time dramatically. If they're going to be sitting around for a bit, leave them in cold water with a splash of lemon juice so that they don't oxidize.

INGREDIENTS

For the Arugula Pesto

1 cup arugula

1 cup spinach

1 garlic clove, minced

⅓ cup pine nuts

2 tablespoons Parmesan cheese, finely grated

3 tablespoons extra virgin olive oil

Salt and pepper, to taste

For the Creamed Parsnip Soup

2 tablespoons unsalted butter

1 onion, chopped

1 garlic clove, minced

2 sprigs thyme, leaves removed and chopped

5 parsnips, peeled and grated

6 cups vegetable stock (see page 25)

2 cups heavy cream

Salt and pepper, to taste

Parsley, chopped, for garnish

1 To make the Arugula Pesto, combine all the ingredients in a food processor and puree until it reaches desired consistency. Season with salt and pepper and serve.

2 In a medium saucepan, add the butter and cook over medium heat until it is melted. Add the onion, garlic, and thyme to the pan and cook for 5 minutes, or until soft. Add the parsnips and cook for 5 minutes.

3 Add the stock and bring to a boil. Reduce the heat so that the soup simmers and cook for 10 minutes.

4 Remove the pan from the heat and transfer to a food processor. Puree the soup until it is smooth and then strain through a fine sieve.

5 Return to the soup to a clean pan, bring to a simmer, and add heavy cream. Simmer for 5 minutes and season with salt and pepper. Ladle into warm bowls, serve with Arugula Pesto, and garnish with parsley.

Creamy Spring Sweet Pea Soup with Crème Fraîche

YIELD: 4 SERVINGS • ACTIVE TIME: 10 MINUTES • TOTAL TIME: 20 MINUTES

This soup can be served hot or cool, and makes a delicious snack or light meal. Use frozen peas to lower the broth's temperature and maintain its lovely green color.

1 In a medium saucepan, add butter and cook over medium heat until melted.

2 Add the leek and onion and cook for 5 minutes, or until soft. Add the vegetable stock and bring to a boil.

3 Reduce heat until the soup simmers. Add the frozen peas and cook for 5 minutes.

4 Remove the pan from heat and add the soup and parsley to a food processor. Puree the soup until it is smooth.

5 Return soup to a clean pan and bring to a simmer. Add crème fraîche, season with salt and pepper, and serve.

INGREDIENTS

2 tablespoons unsalted butter

1 leek, white part only, chopped

1 onion, peeled and chopped

4 cups vegetable stock (see page 25)

1½ lbs. frozen peas

4 sprigs parsley, leaves removed and chopped

1 cup crème fraîche

Salt and pepper, to taste

Korean Beef and Rice Soup

YIELD: 4 SERVINGS • ACTIVE TIME: 15 MINUTES • TOTAL TIME: 30 MINUTES

This aromatic, refreshing soup has just a slight bit of heat. It's perfect to enjoy when you're pressed for time.

INGREDIENTS

2 tablespoons vegetable oil

1 lb. boneless beef chuck, cut into ½-inch pieces

2 garlic cloves, minced

8 cups beef stock (see page 12)

1 cup long-grain rice

2 tablespoons sesame seeds

1 teaspoon red chili flakes

1 star anise

1 cinnamon stick

2 tablespoons sesame oil

2 tablespoons fish sauce

2 tablespoons soy sauce

1 tablespoon rice wine vinegar

4 scallions, sliced, greens reserved for garnish

4 celery stalks, chopped

Salt and pepper, to taste

1 In a medium saucepan, add 1 tablespoon of oil and cook over medium-high heat until warm. Add the beef chuck and cook for 3 to 5 minutes, while turning, until nicely browned.

2 Add the garlic, beef stock, and rice, increase temperature to high, and bring to a boil. Reduce heat so that the soup simmers and cook for 15 minutes.

3 Meanwhile, in an ungreased sauté pan, add the sesame seeds, red chili flakes, star anise, and cinnamon stick and cook for 3 minutes over medium heat while stirring often, until the pan gives off a nice aroma.

4 Remove sauté pan from heat and stir in the sesame oil, fish sauce, soy sauce, rice wine vinegar, and the remaining vegetable oil. Set aside to cool.

5 Once the rice in the soup is tender, add the scallion whites and celery and cook for 5 minutes, or until the celery is soft.

6 Season the soup with salt and pepper, serve in warmed bowls, and garnish with the infused oil and scallion greens.

Fennel-Scented Olive and Tomato Soup with Horiatiki Salad

YIELD: 4 SERVINGS • ACTIVE TIME: 15 MINUTES • TOTAL TIME: 30 MINUTES

A quick Mediterranean soup with a Greek side salad. If you have a few minutes, blend the soup to make this a touch more refined.

INGREDIENTS

For the Horiatiki Salad

½ cucumber, peeled, halved lengthwise, seeds removed, and cut into half-moons

½ cup cherry tomatoes, halved

½ cup feta cheese, crumbled

½ onion, peeled and chopped

¼ cup Kalamata olives, pitted and sliced

1 teaspoon dried oregano

¼ cup extra virgin olive oil

Salt and pepper, to taste

For the Fennel-Scented Olive and Tomato Soup

2 tablespoons extra virgin olive oil

1 onion, peeled and chopped

2 garlic cloves, minced

2 fennel bulbs, chopped, fennel fronds reserved for garnish

½ cup Kalamata olives, pitted and chopped

2 sprigs rosemary, leaves removed and chopped

2 sprigs thyme, leaves removed and chopped

1 tablespoon orange zest

1½ tablespoons tomato paste

2 (14 oz.) cans stewed tomatoes

4 cups chicken stock (see page 14)

Salt and pepper, to taste

1 To make the Horiatiki salad, add the cucumber, cherry tomatoes, feta, onion, olives, and dried oregano to a mixing bowl and stir gently until combined.

2 Right before serving, drizzle with the olive oil and season with salt and pepper. Gently toss and set aside.

3 To make the soup, add the olive oil to a medium saucepan and cook over medium heat until warm. Add the onion, garlic, and fennel and cook for 5 minutes, or until soft.

4 Add the remaining ingredients and bring to a boil. Reduce heat so that soup simmers and cook for 12 minutes, or until the vegetables are tender.

5 Season with salt and pepper and ladle into warm bowls. Garnish with the fennel fronds and serve with the Horiatiki.

Lemon Asparagus Soup

YIELD: 4 SERVINGS • ACTIVE TIME: 15 MINUTES • TOTAL TIME: 30 MINUTES

When spring rolls around we are presented with beautiful asparagus. It's a very quick vegetable to cook, making it perfect for this chapter.

INGREDIENTS

For the Grated Parmesan with Lemon Zest and Parsley

½ cup Parmesan cheese, grated

2 tablespoons lemon zest

2 tablespoons parsley, leaves removed and chopped

For the Lemon Asparagus Soup

2 tablespoons unsalted butter

1 leek, chopped

1½ lbs. green asparagus, peeled and chopped

5 cups of vegetable stock (see page 25)

½ cup heavy cream

Zest of 2 lemons

Salt and pepper, to taste

1 To prepare the Grated Parmesan with Lemon Zest and Parsley, add the ingredients to a bowl and stir until combined.

2 To make the soup, add the butter to a medium saucepan and cook over medium heat until melted. Add the leek and cook for 5 minutes, or until soft.

3 Add the asparagus. Add the vegetable stock and bring to a boil. Reduce the heat so that the soup simmers and cook for 6 to 8 minutes, or until the vegetables are tender.

4 Remove the pan from heat and transfer the soup to a food processor. Blend until smooth and then pass through a fine sieve.

5 Return soup to a clean pan and add cream and lemon zest. Season with salt and pepper and bring to a simmer. Serve in warmed bowls with Grated Parmesan with Lemon Zest and Parsley.

Moroccan Chickpea Stew with Carrot and Mint Salad

YIELD: 4 SERVINGS • ACTIVE TIME: 15 MINUTES • TOTAL TIME: 30 MINUTES

This classic Moroccan soup will make your day—particularly when served alongside a refreshing carrot and mint salad.

INGREDIENTS

For the Moroccan Chickpea Stew

2 tablespoons extra virgin olive oil

1 onion, chopped

2 carrots, peeled and grated

1 teaspoon ground coriander

1 teaspoon cumin

2 cinnamon sticks

4 cups veal stock (see page 12)

2 garlic cloves, minced

2 (14 oz.) cans stewed tomatoes, chopped

1 tablespoon tomato paste

1 (14 oz.) can chickpeas, drained

Salt and pepper, to taste

For the Carrot and Mint Salad

2 carrots, peeled and grated

1 tablespoon extra virgin olive oil

2 teaspoons apple cider vinegar

½ teaspoon cumin

1 tablespoon mint, leaves removed and chopped

Salt and pepper, to taste

1 To make the stew, add the oil to a medium saucepan and cook over medium heat. When the oil is warm, add the onion and carrots and cook for 5 minutes, or until soft.

2 Add the spices and cook for 2 minutes. Add the veal stock, garlic, tomatoes, and tomato paste and bring to a boil. Add the chickpeas and reduce heat so that the soup simmers.

3 While the soup simmers, make the Carrot and Mint Salad by combining all ingredients in a bowl and mixing gently.

4 After 5 minutes, season the soup with salt and pepper and serve in warmed bowls alongside the Carrot and Mint Salad.

Cambodian Chicken and Jasmine Rice Soup with Shrimp

YIELD: 4 SERVINGS • ACTIVE TIME: 15 MINUTES • TOTAL TIME: 30 MINUTES

After a long day at work, it can be brutal thinking up something everyone will love. With this soup, and an assist from a rotisserie chicken from the grocery store, you now have nothing to fear.

INGREDIENTS

1 (3-lb.) rotisserie chicken, legs and breasts removed

1 tablespoon vegetable oil

2 tablespoons ginger, minced

2 garlic cloves, minced

6 cups chicken stock (see page 14)

3 tablespoons fish sauce

1 teaspoon honey

1 cup cooked jasmine rice

12 shrimp, shelled, deveined, and halved

2 tablespoons lime juice

¼ cup cilantro, chopped

2 tablespoons basil, chopped

1 Thai chili, seeds removed and sliced

Salt and pepper, to taste

Lime wedges, for garnish

1 Cut the chicken breasts into 1½-inch pieces, and remove the meat from the thighs and drumsticks. In a medium saucepan, add the vegetable oil and cook over medium heat until warm.

2 Add the ginger and garlic and cook for 3 minutes, or until soft. Add the stock, fish sauce, honey, and cooked rice and bring to a boil.

3 Reduce heat so that the soup simmers, add the chicken pieces, and cook for 5 minutes. Add the shrimp and simmer for 2 minutes.

4 Stir in the lime juice, cilantro, basil, and Thai chili. Season with salt and pepper and serve in warmed bowls with lime wedges.

Pasta e Fagioli

YIELD: 4 SERVINGS • ACTIVE TIME: 15 MINUTES • TOTAL TIME: 30 MINUTES

Like many other Italian favorites, including pizza and polenta, this started out as a peasant dish, and is composed of inexpensive ingredients.

INGREDIENTS

For the Mediterranean Herbs

1 tablespoon dried rosemary

2 teaspoons cumin

2 teaspoons ground coriander

1 teaspoon dried oregano

⅛ teaspoon salt

For the Pasta e Fagioli

2 tablespoons extra virgin olive oil

1 onion, peeled and chopped

2 carrots, peeled and grated

2 celery stalks, chopped

1 garlic clove, minced

4 cups chicken stock (see page 14)

1 (14 oz.) can stewed tomatoes, chopped

2 tablespoons Mediterranean Herbs

1 cup elbow pasta

1 (14 oz.) can pinto beans

Salt and pepper, to taste

1 cup Parmesan cheese, shaved, for garnish

1 To make the Mediterranean Herbs, add all ingredients together in a small bowl and then store in an airtight container until ready to use.

2 For the Pasta e Fagioli, add oil to a medium saucepan and cook over medium heat. When the oil is warm, add onion, carrots, celery, and garlic and cook for 5 minutes, or until soft.

3 Add the stock, tomatoes, and Mediterranean Herbs and bring to a boil. Reduce heat so that soup simmers, add elbow pasta, and cook for 10 minutes. Add the pinto beans and cook for an additional 5 minutes.

4 Season with salt and pepper, garnish with Parmesan cheese, and serve in warmed bowls.

Quick Lamb Stew

YIELD: 4 SERVINGS • ACTIVE TIME: 15 MINUTES • TOTAL TIME: 30 MINUTES

Want to put together a hearty meal for the whole family, but crunched for time? This quick lamb stew will come to the rescue.

INGREDIENTS

2 tablespoons vegetable oil

1 onion, peeled and chopped

1 lb. lamb loin, fat removed and cut into ½-inch pieces

2 garlic cloves, chopped

1 tablespoon cumin

1 tablespoon rosemary, leaves removed and chopped, plus 4 sprigs for garnish

2 (14 oz.) cans diced tomatoes

4 cups lamb stock (see page 12)

2 potatoes, peeled and cut into ½-inch pieces

2 cups green beans, chopped

Juice of 1 lemon

Salt and pepper, to taste

1 In a medium saucepan, add the oil and cook over medium heat. When the oil is warm, add the onion and lamb and cook for 5 minutes, or until lamb is browned all over.

2 Add the garlic, cumin, rosemary, and tomatoes and cook for an additional 5 minutes. Add the stock and potatoes, increase heat to high, and bring to a boil.

3 Reduce heat so that the soup simmers. Cook for 10 minutes, or until the potatoes are tender. Add the green beans and cook for 5 minutes.

4 Season with lemon juice, salt, and pepper and serve in warmed bowls garnished with a sprig of rosemary.

Semi-Homemade Ramen

YIELD: 4 SERVINGS • ACTIVE TIME: 15 MINUTES • TOTAL TIME: 30 MINUTES

Pull out the ramen, throw out the seasoning packet, and make this grownup version of your old college standby.

INGREDIENTS

2 tablespoons sesame oil

2 chicken breasts, skin removed and chopped into ½-inch pieces

1 onion, peeled and chopped

1-inch piece ginger

2 garlic cloves, chopped

¼ teaspoon red chili flakes

4 tablespoons soy sauce, or to taste

8 cups chicken stock (see page 14)

Noodles from 4 packets of ramen

4 Poached Eggs (see page 57)

Salt and pepper, to taste

4 scallions, sliced, greens reserved for garnish

Bean sprouts, for garnish

1 In a medium saucepan, add the sesame oil and cook over medium heat. When the oil is warm, add the chicken and cook, while turning, for 5 minutes.

3 Add the onion, ginger, garlic cloves, and chili flakes and cook for an additional 5 minutes. Add the soy sauce and stock and bring to a boil. Reduce the heat so that the soup simmers and cook for 10 minutes.

3 Add the ramen noodles and cook for 5 additional minutes. When the noodles are cooking, prepare your Poached Eggs.

4 Divide the soup between four bowls, add the Poached Eggs, season to taste, garnish with the scallion greens and bean sprouts, and serve.

Smoked Chorizo and Cabbage Soup

YIELD: 4 SERVINGS • ACTIVE TIME: 15 MINUTES • TOTAL TIME: 30 MINUTES

This soup is a great use of European ingredients and techniques!

INGREDIENTS

2 tablespoons extra virgin olive oil

1 onion, chopped

4 sprigs thyme, leaves removed and chopped

1 lb. dried smoked chorizo, sliced into ¼-inch pieces

1 green cabbage, halved, core removed, and cut into ¼-inch slices

1 tablespoon cumin seeds

1 cinnamon stick

6 cups chicken stock (see page 14)

Salt and pepper, to taste

1 In a medium saucepan, add the oil and cook over medium heat. When the oil is warm, add the onion and cook for 5 minutes, or until soft.

2 Add the thyme, chorizo, cabbage, cumin seeds, and cinnamon stick, cover, and cook for 5 minutes, stirring occasionally. Add the stock, raise the heat to high, and bring to a boil.

3 Reduce heat so that the soup simmers and cook for an additional 10 minutes. Season with salt and pepper and serve in warmed bowls.

Sausage, Spinach, and Bean Soup

YIELD: 4 SERVINGS • ACTIVE TIME: 15 MINUTES • TOTAL TIME: 30 MINUTES

It seems impossible that a soup this tasty could take anything less than a day to make.

INGREDIENTS

2 tablespoons extra virgin olive oil

1 lb. hot Italian sausage, cut into ½-inch slices

2 garlic cloves, minced

½ teaspoon red chili flakes

1 lb. baby spinach

1 (14 oz.) can cannellini beans, rinsed, drained, and cooked

6 cups chicken stock (see page 14)

1 bay leaf

Salt and pepper, to taste

1 cup Parmesan cheese, grated, for garnish

1 In a medium saucepan, add the oil and cook over medium heat. When the oil is warm, add the sausage and cook for 3 to 5 minutes, while turning, until nicely browned.

2 Add the garlic, chili flakes, and baby spinach, cover, and cook, stirring frequently until the spinach is wilted, approximately 5 minutes. Add the beans, stock, and bay leaf, increase the heat to high, and bring to a boil.

3 Reduce heat so that the soup simmers and cook for 10 minutes. Remove the bay leaf, season soup with salt and pepper, and serve in warmed bowls with a sprinkle of Parmesan.

Thai Chicken and Coconut Soup

YIELD: 4 SERVINGS • ACTIVE TIME: 15 MINUTES • TOTAL TIME: 30 MINUTES

This refreshing, spicy soup is perfect for the end of a cold day.

INGREDIENTS

2 tablespoons vegetable oil

2 chicken breasts, skin removed, chopped into ½-inch pieces

1 onion, peeled and chopped

4 cups chicken stock (see page 14)

2-inch piece ginger, peeled and minced

2 Thai chilies, seeds removed, 1 diced, 1 sliced and reserved for garnish

2 lemongrass stalks, halved and bruised with the back of a knifo

4 carrots, peeled and chopped

2 (14 oz. cans) coconut milk

3 tablespoons fish sauce

Juice of 1 lime

Salt and pepper, to taste

Thai basil leaves, for garnish

1 In a medium saucepan, add the oil and cook over medium heat. When the oil is warm, add the chicken and onion and cook for 5 minutes, or until chicken is browned.

2 Add the stock, ginger, diced Thai chili, lemongrass, and carrots. Increase the heat to high and bring to a boil.

3 Reduce heat so that the soup simmers. Cook for 5 minutes and then add the coconut milk. Simmer for an additional 5 minutes, or until the carrots are soft.

4 Remove the lemongrass and add fish sauce, lime juice, salt, and pepper. Serve in warm bowls and garnish with sliced Thai chili and Thai basil.

Quick Kimchi Ramen

YIELD: 4 SERVINGS • ACTIVE TIME: 10 MINUTES • TOTAL TIME: 30 MINUTES

The out-of-this-world flavor in this soup is thanks to the kimchi. Feel free to make your own; it's typically ready in under a week.

INGREDIENTS

¼ cup vegetable oil

2 shiitake mushrooms, thinly sliced

2 cups kimchi, chopped

1 cup kimchi juice

6 cups chicken stock (see page 14)

½ teaspoon chili powder, or to taste

1 teaspoon sugar

1 tablespoon sesame oil

Salt and pepper, to taste

Noodles from 2 packets of ramen

4 scallions, sliced, for garnish

1 In a medium saucepan, add the vegetable oil and cook over medium-high heat until warm. Add the shiitakes to the pan and cook for 3 minutes.

2 Add the kimchi, kimchi juice, chicken stock, chili powder, sugar, and sesame oil and bring to a boil. Reduce heat so that the soup simmers, cook for 5 minutes, and then season with salt and pepper.

3 Cook ramen noodles per manufacturer's instructions. Divide them between four bowls and then pour the broth over them. Garnish with scallions and serve.

Tom Yum Koong Soup

This soup has a very aromatic citrus smell and flavor. It is meant to be spicy, so make sure you tailor the amount of chilies and curry paste to your taste.

INGREDIENTS

6 cups chicken stock
(see page 14)

2 lemongrass stalks,
bruised with the back of a knife

2-inch piece of galangal root

4 kaffir lime leaves

2 Thai chilies, seeds removed and sliced

2 tablespoons fish sauce

Juice of 3 limes

1½ teaspoons sugar

1 tablespoon Thai red curry paste

12 oz. shrimp, peeled and deveined

24 shiitake mushrooms, halved

Salt and pepper, to taste

Cilantro leaves, for garnish

1 In a large saucepan, combine the chicken stock, lemongrass, galangal root, lime leaves, chilies, fish sauce, lime juice, sugar, and curry paste. Bring to a boil, reduce the heat so that the soup simmers, and cook for 5 minutes.

2 Strain the soup through a fine sieve and return to a clean pan. Turn off heat and let stand for 20 minutes.

3 Bring soup to a simmer. Add shrimp and mushrooms and cook for 5 minutes.

4 Season with salt and pepper. Serve in warmed bowls garnished with cilantro leaves.

Chilled Maine Blueberry and Yogurt Soup

YIELD: 4 SERVINGS • ACTIVE TIME: 5 MINUTES • TOTAL TIME: 30 MINUTES

Enjoy this refreshing Maine staple on a warm summer day.

1 Place all ingredients in a food processor and gently pulse until combined.

2 Season with sugar to taste and place in the refrigerator for 15 minutes.

3 Serve in chilled bowls, or Champagne flutes, with fresh blueberries.

INGREDIENTS

2 cups Maine blueberries, plus more for garnish

4 cups Greek yogurt

1 cup orange juice

1 cup Champagne

1 vanilla bean, scraped

1 teaspoon cinnamon

Sugar, to taste

Chilled Mango Soup

YIELD: 4 SERVINGS • ACTIVE TIME: 5 MINUTES • TOTAL TIME: 25 MINUTES

Want a healthy snack or light finish to a warm summer day? Try this delicious, fruity soup.

INGREDIENTS

2 large ripe mangos, peeled and diced

2 cups orange juice

2 teaspoons honey, or to taste

1 cup yogurt

Mint leaves, for garnish

Blood orange segments, for garnish

Fresh kiwi, for garnish

1 In a food processor, combine the mango, orange juice, honey, and yogurt. Puree until smooth and chill in the refrigerator for 20 minutes.

2 Remove from refrigerator, serve in chilled bowls, and garnish with mint leaves, blood orange segments, and fresh kiwi.

White Chocolate Soup

YIELD: 4 SERVINGS • ACTIVE TIME: 10 MINUTES • TOTAL TIME: 25 MINUTES

Whip up this one for a special treat after dinner, or for watching a movie.

1 In a medium saucepan, add the milk, cream, vanilla pod, and the vanilla bean seeds and bring to a simmer over medium heat.

2 Turn off heat and let sit for 10 minutes.

3 Remove vanilla pod and return to a simmer. When the soup is simmering, turn off heat.

4 Add chocolate and whisk until melted. Strain soup through a fine sieve and then serve in coffee cups garnished with fresh mint.

INGREDIENTS

3 cups milk

1 cup heavy cream

1 vanilla bean, scraped

1 lb. white chocolate

Mint leaves, for garnish

Metric Equivalents

Weights

1 ounce	28 grams
2 ounces	57 grams
4 ounces (¼ pound)	113 grams
8 ounces (½ pound)	227 grams
16 ounces (1 pound)	454 grams

Volume Measures

⅛ teaspoon		0.6 ml
¼ teaspoon		1.23 ml
½ teaspoon		2.5 ml
1 teaspoon		5 ml
1 tablespoon (3 teaspoons)	½ fluid ounce	15 ml
2 tablespoons	1 fluid ounce	29.5 ml
¼ cup (4 tablespoons)	2 fluid ounces	59 ml
⅓ cup (5⅓ tablespoons)	2.7 fluid ounces	80 ml
½ cup (8 tablespoons)	4 fluid ounces	120 ml
⅔ cup (10⅔ tablespoons)	5.4 fluid ounces	160 ml
¾ cup (12 tablespoons)	6 fluid ounces	180 ml
1 cup (16 tablespoons)	8 fluid ounces	240 ml

Temperature Equivalents

°F	°C	Gas Mark
225	110	¼
250	130	½
275	140	1
300	150	2
325	170	3
350	180	4
375	190	5
400	200	6
425	220	7
450	230	8
475	240	9
500	250	10

Length Measures

1⁄16-inch	1.6 mm
⅛-inch	3 mm
¼-inch	0.63 cm
½-inch	1.25 cm
¾-inch	2 cm
1-inch	2.5 cm

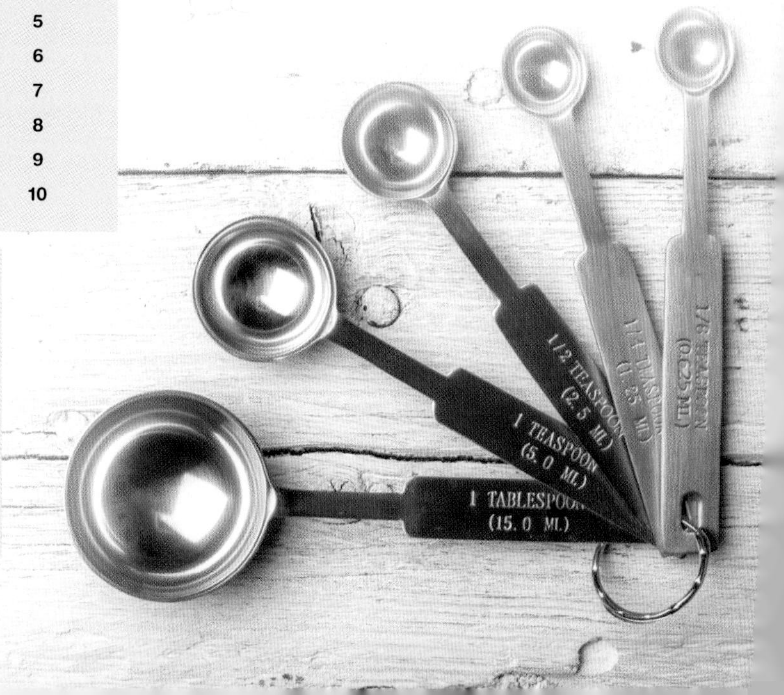

Index

About the Author

Derek Bissonnette has been a chef for the past 22 years, and is the former Executive Chef at the White Barn Inn in Kennebunk, Maine. He stepped out of the kitchen to focus on his passion for photography and opened up Derek Bissonnette Photography. Visit him online at dbmainephotography.com.

ABOUT CIDER MILL PRESS BOOK PUBLISHERS

Good ideas ripen with time. From seed to harvest, Cider Mill
Press brings fine reading, information, and entertainment
together between the covers of its creatively crafted books.
Our Cider Mill bears fruit twice a year, publishing
a new crop of titles each spring and fall.

"Where Good Books Are Ready for Press"

VISIT US ONLINE:
www.cidermillpress.com

OR WRITE TO US AT
PO Box 454
12 Spring St.
Kennebunkport, Maine 04046